CRIARD, E adj. **1.** Qui crie désagréablement, qui se plaint souvent sans motif sérieux. **2.** Aigu et désagréable : *Voix criarde.* **3.** *Couleurs criardes* : couleurs crues contrastant désagréablement entre elles. **4.** *Dettes criardes,* dont on réclame instamment le paiement.

CRIB n.m. (mot angl.). Cellule grillagée pour le stockage et le séchage en plein air des épis de maïs.

CRIBLAGE n.m. **1.** Action de cribler. **2.** MIN Triage mécanique par grosseur des minerais, de la houille, etc.

CRIBLE n.m. (lat. *cribrum*). Appareil à fond plan perforé, utilisé pour séparer selon leur grosseur des fragments solides (grains, sable, minerais, etc.). ◇ *Passer au crible* : examiner avec soin, trier.

CRIBLER v.t. (lat. *cribrare*). **1.** Passer au crible : *Cribler du sable.* **2.** Percer de trous nombreux ; couvrir de marques : *Être criblé de coups.* ◇ *Être criblé de dettes,* en avoir énormément.

CRIBLEUR n.m. Machine à cribler.

1. CRIC interj. (Se joint souvent à *crac !*) Exprime un bruit sec, un craquement.

2. CRIC n.m. (haut all. *kriec*). Appareil agissant directement par poussée sur un fardeau et permettant de le soulever ou de le déplacer sur une faible course.

CRICKET [kriket] n.m. (mot angl.). Jeu de balle anglais où se joue avec des battes de bois.

CRICOÏDE adj. *Cartilage cricoïde,* ou *cricoïde,* n.m. : anneau cartilagineux de la base du larynx.

CRICRI n.m. (onomat.). *Fam.* **1.** Cri du grillon, de la cigale. **2.** Grillon domestique.

CRIÉE n.f. *Vente à la criée,* ou *criée* : vente publique aux enchères de certaines marchandises. *Criée du poisson sur le port.*

CRIER v.i. [5] (lat. *quiritare*). **1.** Pousser un cri, des cris : *Crier de douleur.* **2.** Parler fort et soutenu avec colère. *Parle sans crier !* ◇ *Crier au scandale, à la trahison,* etc., les dénoncer vigoureusement. — *Crier après, contre qqn,* le réprimander d'une voix forte. **3.** Produire un bruit aigre : grincer, crisser. *Faire crier la craie sur le tableau.* **4.** Produire un effet désagréable à l'œil. *Un vert qui crie.* ◆ v.t. **1.** Dire à haute voix : *Crier un ordre.* **2.** Manifester énergiquement un sentiment, une opinion : *Crier son indignation.* ◇ *Crier famine, misère* : se plaindre de la faim, de la misère. — *Crier vengeance* : mériter une vengeance ; demander réparation. *Un forfait qui crie vengeance.*

CRIEUR, EUSE n. **1.** Personne qui annonce en criant la vente d'une marchandise. *Crieur de journaux.* **2.** Anc. *Crieur public* : préposé aux proclamations publiques.

CRIME n.m. (lat. *crimen,* accusation). **1.** Meurtre, assassinat. **2.** DR Infraction que la loi punit d'une peine afflictive et infamante ou simplement infamante. **3.** *Crime de guerre* : violation des lois et coutumes de la guerre (pillage, assassinat, exécution d'otages). — *Crime contre l'humanité* : exécution d'un plan concerté (génocide, déportation, extermination, réduction en esclavage) inspiré par des motifs politiques, philosophiques, raciaux ou religieux, perpétré à l'encontre de tout ou partie d'un groupe de population. Cf.info. **4.** Acte répréhensible, fond de conséquences. ENCYCL. Les crimes de guerre ou contre l'humanité sont des crimes de droit international définis en 1945 par l'Organisation des Nations unies. Les crimes contre l'humanité sont imprescriptibles. Ceux qui ont été commis pendant la Seconde Guerre mondiale furent jugés par le Tribunal international de Nuremberg.

CRIMINALISER v.t. DR Faire passer de la juridiction correctionnelle (ou civile) à la juridiction criminelle.

CRIMINALISTE n. Juriste spécialiste en matière criminelle.

CRIMINALISTIQUE n.f. Ensemble des techniques permettant d'aider la justice, pour établir la preuve d'un crime et d'en identifier l'auteur.

CRIMINALITÉ n.f. Ensemble des actes criminels et délictueux entraînant dans un groupe donné, à une époque donnée, la délinquance en général et la fraude.

CRIMINEL, ELLE adj. et n. Coupable d'un crime. ◆ adj. **1.** Contraire aux prescriptions de la loi : *Acte criminel.* **2.** DR Relatif aux crimes : *Droit criminel.* ◆ n.m. DR *Le criminel* : la matière criminelle ; sa juridiction active.

CRIMINELLEMENT adv. **1.** De façon criminelle. **2.** DR Devant la juridiction criminelle.

CRIMINOGÈNE adj. Qui peut engendrer des actes criminels.

CRIMINOLOGIE n.f. Étude scientifique du phénomène criminel.

CRIMINOLOGISTE ou **CRIMINOLOGUE** n. Spécialiste de criminologie.

CRIN n.m. (lat. *crinis,* cheveu). **1.** Poil long et rude qui pousse sur le cou et à la queue des chevaux et de quelques autres quadrupèdes. — Ce poil dans ses diverses utilisations (balais, pinceaux, archets, etc.). ◇ *Fam. À tous crins* : à outrance. **2.** BOT. *Crin végétal* : matière filamenteuse extraite du palmier, de l'agave, etc.

CRINCRIN n.m. (onomat.). *Fam.* Mauvais violon.

CRINIÈRE n.f. **1.** Ensemble des crins du cou d'un cheval, d'un lion. **2.** Touffe de crins ornant le haut d'un casque et retombant par-derrière. **3.** *Fam.* Chevelure abondante.

CRINOÏDE n.m. Échinoderme constitué d'un calice entouré de cinq paires de bras, dont certaines espèces, telles les encrines, se fixent au fond de la mer par un pédoncule articulé. (Les fragments fossiles de crinoïdes ont formé le calcaire dit *à entroques.* Les crinoïdes forment une classe.)

CRINOLINE n.f. (ital. *crinolino,* de *crino,* crin, et *lino,* lin). Anc. Armature de cerceaux métalliques superposés qui donnait une grande ampleur à la jupe des robes. (Fabriquée à partir de 1850, elle a été utilisée jusqu'en 1869, où elle a fait place à la tournure.) *Robe à crinoline,* ou *crinoline.*

CRIOCÈRE n.m. (gr. *krios,* bélier, et *keras,* corne). Insecte coléoptère, dont une espèce rouge attaque les lis et une autre, bleu et jaune, vit sur l'asperge. (Long. moins de 1 cm ; famille des chrysomélidés.)

CRIQUE n.f. (scand. *kriki*). **1.** Petite baie, petite anse du littoral. **2.** MÉTALL. Fente ouverte en surface, qui se produit dans un métal, due à la séparation entre grains sous l'effet de contraintes anormales.

CRIQUET n.m. (onomat.). Insecte orthoptère sauteur, aux antennes courtes, végétarien, dont certaines espèces des régions chaudes pullulent périodiquement et migrent alors en immenses nuées dévastatrices. (Famille des acridiés.)

■ **CRIQUET.** Criquet migrateur.

CRISE n.f. (gr. *krisis,* décision). **1. a.** Changement subit, souvent décisif, favorable ou défavorable, du cours d'une maladie. **b.** Manifestation soudaine ou aggravation brutale d'un état morbide. *Crise cardiaque.* *Crise de rhumatismes.* **2.** Accès bref et violent d'un état nerveux, ou émotif : *Crise de nerfs* : état d'agitation bref et soudain avec cris et gesticulation. **3.** *Fam.* Accès soudain d'ardeur, d'enthousiasme. *Travailler par crises.* **4.** Période décisive ou périlleuse de l'existence. **5.** *Crise biologique* : période de l'histoire des êtres vivants caractérisée par des extinctions massives et brutales. (Les deux crises biologiques les plus importantes sont celles de la fin du permien et de la fin du crétacé.) **6. a.** Phase difficile traversée par un groupe social. *Crise de l'Université.* **b.** *Crise économique* : rupture d'équilibre entre grandeurs économiques, notamment entre production et consommation. **c.** *Crise ministérielle* : situation qui débute par l'exécutif est obligé à la démission, et se maintient pendant la formation du nouveau. **7.** Crise pénurie, insuffisance. *Crise de la main-d'œuvre, du logement.* ENCYCL. Jusqu'au milieu du XIXe s., les crises se manifestaient sous forme de *crises de sous-production,* analogues à celles de l'Ancien Régime : elles avaient alors des causes naturelles. Puis le développement de l'industrie marque la généralisation à partir de l'introduction des systèmes économiques. La *crise* de surproduction inaugurées, bien dégagée avec l'avènement industriel. Dans un système reposant sur la concurrence et sur la libre entreprise, ces crises se traduisent par une chute de la production et des prix. La crise matérielle fut la crise de 1929, dont seule la Seconde Guerre mondiale permit de sortir. Depuis 1974, une série...

du quadruplement du prix du pétrole, présente des aspects originaux : sa longueur et la simultanéité de phénomènes jusqu'alors antinomiques, comme le chômage coexistant avec l'inflation (*stagflation*). En octobre 1987, le marché boursier international connaît un nouveau krach de grande ampleur, conséquence directe d'une spéculation financière et reflet de la précarité monétaire internationale. En 1991, une nouvelle crise, liée à la guerre du Golfe, secoue l'économie mondiale. En 1997, un autre krach boursier touchant les principaux pays d'Asie (dont le Japon) a des répercussions sur toutes les places financières, ralentissant la reprise économique mondiale.

CRISPANT, E adj. Qui agace vivement ; horripilant.

CRISPATION n.f. **1.** Contraction musculaire provoquée par la nervosité, la peur. **2.** Mouvement d'impatience, d'irritation, de nervosité. **3.** Contraction qui plisse la surface de certaines matières souples.

CRISPER v.t. (lat. *crispare,* rider). **1.** Contracter les muscles. **2.** Causer de l'agacement ; irriter. **3.** Donner un aspect ridé à la surface de certains matériaux. ◆ **se crisper** v.pr. **1.** Se contracter vivement. **2.** Éprouver une vive irritation.

CRISPIN n.m. (ital. *Crispino,* n. d'un valet de comédie). Manchette de cuir adaptée à certains gants d'escrimeur, de motocycliste, etc.

CRISS ou n. → KRISS.

CRISSEMENT n.m. Grincement aigu.

CRISSER v.i. (onomat.). Produire un bruit aigu, grinçant.

CRISTAL n.m. [pl. *cristaux*] (lat. *crystallus,* mot gr.). **1. a.** Corps solide pouvant affecter une forme géométrique bien définie et caractérisé par une répartition régulière et périodique des atomes. **b.** *Cristal de roche* : quartz hyalin et incolore, utilisé en joaillerie et autres arts appliqués. *Cristal liquide* : liquide à l'état mésomorphe, utilisé notamment pour les fonctions d'affichage. SYN *corps mésomorphe.* **2.** Verre à l'oxyde de plomb très limpide et sonore. ◆ pl. **1.** Vieilli. Carbonate de sodium cristallise utilisé pour le nettoyage. **2.** Objets en cristal.

CRISTALLERIE n.f. Fabrication d'objets en cristal ; établissement où ils sont fabriqués.

1. CRISTALLIN, E adj. **1. a.** De la nature du cristal. **b.** *Roche cristalline* : roche constituée de cristaux visibles à l'œil nu et formée, en profondeur, à partir d'un magma (roche plutonique) ou par recristallisation à l'état solide (roche métamorphique). **c.** *Système cristallin* : ensemble des éléments de symétrie caractéristiques du réseau d'un cristal. (Il y a sept systèmes cristallins : triclinique, monoclinique, orthorhombique, quadratique, cubique, rhomboédrique, hexagonal.) **2.** *Fig* Semblable au cristal par la transparence ou la sonorité. *Eaux cristallines. Voix cristalline.*

2. CRISTALLIN n.m. Élément de l'œil, en forme de lentille biconvexe, situé dans le globe oculaire en arrière de l'iris et permettant à l'accommodation.

CRISTALLINIEN, ENNE adj. Relatif au cristallin.

CRISTALLISABLE adj. Susceptible de se former en cristaux.

CRISTALLISANT, E adj. Qui détermine la cristallisation, la formation de cristaux.

CRISTALLISATION n.f. **1.** Changement d'état d'un matériau conduisant à la formation de cristaux. **2.** Amas de cristaux, de minéraux affectant des formes polyédriques. **3.** *Litt.* Fait de se cristalliser, de prendre corps. *Cristallisation amoureuse.*

CRISTALLISÉ, E adj. Qui se présente sous forme de cristaux. *Sucre cristallisé.*

CRISTALLISER v.t. (de *cristal*). **1.** Changer en cristaux. *Cristalliser du sucre.* **2.** *Fig* Donner de la cohésion, de la force à : *Cristalliser ses énergies.* ◆ v.i. ou **se cristalliser** v.pr. **1.** Se former en cristaux. **2.** *Fig* Devenir cohérent en prenant corps. *Souvenirs, sentiments qui se cristallisent.*

CRISTALLISOIR n.m. Récipient de laboratoire, en verre épais à paroi verticale et peu profond, utilisé pour faire cristalliser les corps dissous.

CRISTALLITE n.f. GÉOL Très petit cristal.

CRISTALLOCHIMIE n.f. Branche de la chimie qui étudie les réseaux cristallins.

CRISTALLOGÉNÈSE n.f. Formation des cristaux.

CRISTALLOGRAPHIE n.f. Spécialité de la cristallographie.

CRISTALLOGRAPHIE n.f. Étude scientifique des cristaux et des lois qui président à leur formation.
CRISTALLOGRAPHIQUE adj. Propre à la cristallographie.
CRISTALLOMANCIE n.f. Divination au moyen d'objets de verre ou de cristal.
CRISTALLOPHYLLIEN, ENNE adj. GÉOL. Se dit d'une roche cristalline présentant des feuillets riches en silicates du type mica.
CRISTE-MARINE n.f. [pl. cristes-marines] (lat. crista, du gr. kréthmon, crête marine). Plante à feuilles charnues, comestibles, croissant sur les rochers (d'où son nom de perce-pierre) et les sables littoraux de l'Atlantique. (Genre Crithmum ; famille des ombellifères.)
CRISTOPHINE n.f. Antilles. Cucurbitacée dont la racine et le fruit sont comestibles.
CRITÈRE n.m. (gr. kriterion, de krinein, juger). **1.** Caractère, principe qui permet de distinguer une chose d'une autre, d'émettre un jugement, une estimation. **2.** MATH. Méthode pratique permettant de vérifier si un objet mathématique possède ou non une propriété déterminée.
CRITÉRIUM [kriterjɔm] n.m. (lat. criterium). Nom donné à certaines compétitions sportives, notamm. cyclistes.
CRITICAILLER v.t. Fam., péjor. Critiquer mesquinement.
CRITICISME n.m. Système philosophique de Kant, fondé sur la critique de la connaissance.
CRITIQUABLE adj. Qui peut être critiqué.
1. CRITIQUE adj. (bas lat. criticus, du gr. kritikos, de krinein, juger). **1.** MÉD. Propre à la crise d'une maladie. **2.** Où une décision s'impose ; décisif. Être dans une situation critique. **3.** PHYS. Où se produit un changement dans les propriétés d'un corps, l'allure d'un phénomène. Masse,

gavial : 5 à 7 m

crocodile du Nil : 4 à 6 m

alligator : 3 à 5 m

caïman : 2 m

parties antérieures vues de dessous

■ CROCODILIENS

cubique
$a = b = c$
$\alpha = \beta = \gamma = \frac{\pi}{2}$

quadratique
$a = b \neq c$
$\alpha = \beta = \gamma = \frac{\pi}{2}$

orthorhombique
$a \neq b \neq c$
$\alpha = \beta = \gamma = \frac{\pi}{2}$

monoclinique
$a \neq b \neq c$
$\alpha = \beta = \frac{\pi}{2} \neq \gamma$

triclinique
$a \neq b \neq c$
$\alpha \neq \beta \neq \gamma \neq \frac{\pi}{2}$

rhomboédrique
$a = b = c$
$\alpha = \beta = \gamma \neq \frac{\pi}{2}$

hexagonal
$a = b \neq c$
$\alpha = \beta = \frac{\pi}{2}$

■ CRISTALLIN. Les sept systèmes cristallins.

température critique. **4.** Relatif à la critique, au sens kantien.
2. CRITIQUE n.f. (gr. kriné, de krinein, juger). **1.** Appréciation de l'authenticité d'une chose, de la valeur d'un texte. Critique interne, historique. **2.** Art d'analyser et de juger une œuvre littéraire ou artistique. Critique dramatique, musicale. — Jugement porté sur une œuvre. Roman qui a une bonne critique. **3.** Ensemble des personnes qui, dans les médias, font métier de juger, de commenter une œuvre. Rallier l'unanimité de la critique. **4.** Blâme, reproche porté sur qqn ou qqch. Ne pas supporter la critique. **5.** Chez Kant, examen des pouvoirs de la raison, des conditions de possibilité de la connaissance.
3. CRITIQUE adj. (de 2 critique). **1.** Qui a pour objet de distinguer les qualités ou les défauts d'une œuvre littéraire ou artistique. Analyse critique. — Édition critique : édition établie après collation des différents manuscrits et des différentes éditions d'une même œuvre dont toutes les variantes sont signalées et datées. **2.** Esprit critique : esprit de libre examen ou prompt à blâmer.
4. CRITIQUE n. Personne dont le métier consiste à commenter, à juger des œuvres littéraires ou artistiques, notamm. dans les médias.
CRITIQUER v.t. **1.** Procéder à une analyse critique. **2.** Juger de façon défavorable et souvent malveillante.
CRITIQUEUR, EUSE n. Personne portée à la critique le plus souvent malveillante.
CROASSEMENT n.m. Cri du corbeau.
CROASSER v.i. (onomat.). Pousser son cri, en parlant du corbeau.
CROATE adj. et n. De la Croatie, de ses habitants.
◆ n.m. Langue slave parlée en Croatie.
CROBARD ou **CROBAR** n.m. Fam. Croquis.
CROC [krɔ] n.m. (mot germ.). **1.** Instrument muni d'une ou de plusieurs tiges pointues et recourbées servant à suspendre qqch. **2.** Perche armée d'une extrémité d'un crochet. **3.** ZOOL. Chacune des quatre canines, fortes, longues et pointues, des carnivores. — Fam. Avoir les crocs : avoir faim.
CROC-EN-JAMBE [krɔkɑ̃ʒɑ̃b] n.m. (pl. crocs-en-jambe (krɔkɑ̃-)). **1.** Action d'accrocher du pied une jambe de qqn de manière à le déséquilibrer. SYN. : croche-pied. **2.** Fig. Manœuvre déloyale pour nuire à qqn.
1. CROCHE n.f. MUS. Note valant le huitième d'une ronde, dont la hampe porte un crochet, en position isolée.
2. CROCHE adj. Québec. Fam. **1.** Courbe, recourbé, tordu. Avoir le dos croche. **2.** Fig. Malhonnête. Des gens croches.
CROCHE-PIED ou fam. **CROCHE-PATTE** n.m. (pl. croche-pieds, croche-pattes). Croc-en-jambe.
CROCHER v.t. (de croc). MAR. Accrocher, saisir avec un croc, une gaffe. ◆ v.i. Suisse. Entreprendre à accrocher.
CROCHET n.m. (de croc). **1.** Morceau de métal recourbé servant à suspendre, à fixer ou à tirer à soi qqch. Crochet à décrocher les tableaux. **a.** Instrument à bout recourbé. Crochet de serrurier, de dentiste. **c.** Tige rigide à pointe recourbée utilisée pour faire du tricot, de la dentelle ; travail ainsi exécuté. Faire du crochet. **d.** Dont des serpents venimeux, à extrémité recourbée, qui leur permet d'inoculer le venin à leur proie. **2.** Signe graphique proche de la parenthèse [ ]. **3.** ARCHIT. Ornement en forme de crosse végétale, de bourgeon recourbé (chapiteaux gothiques). **4.** Changement de direction ; détour. Faire un crochet pour aller visiter un monument. **5.** En boxe, coup de poing porté en décrivant une courbe avec le bras. — Au football et au rugby, changement brutal de direction du possesseur du ballon. ◆ pl. **1.** Vx. Châssis du portefaix. **2.** Vivre aux crochets de qqn : à ses frais, à ses dépens.
CROCHETABLE adj. Que l'on peut crocheter. Serrure crochetable.
CROCHETAGE n.m. Action de crocheter une serrure.
CROCHETER v.t. [12]. Ouvrir une serrure une porte avec un crochet.
CROCHETEUR n.m. Vx. Portefaix. Les crocheteurs du Port-au-Foin.
CROCHEUR, EUSE adj. et n. (de crocher). Suisse. Tenace, travailleur.
CROCHU, E adj. Recourbé en forme de crochet, de croc. Bec, nez crochu. — Fam. Avoir les doigts crochus : être avide, avare ou voleur.
CROCO n.m. Fam. Peau tannée du crocodile.
CROCODILE n.m. (lat. crocodilus). **1.** Grand reptile à fortes mâchoires, qui vit dans les fleuves et les lacs des régions tropicales et équatoriales. (Long. jusqu'à 8 m ; en l'ex : le crocodile vit à l'ordre des crocodiliens.) **2.** Peau tannée du crocodile. **3.** CH. DE FER. Point métallique placé entre les rails dans l'axe d'une voie, en avant d'un signal et destiné à déclencher dans la cabine du conducteur la répétition, sous forme sonore, des indications données par ce signal.
CROCODILIEN n.m. Grand reptile aquatique et quadrupède, muni d'une puissante mâchoire. (Les crocodiliens forment un ordre.)
CROCUS [krɔkys] n.m. (mot lat., du gr. krokos, safran). Plante à bulbe et à fleurs isolées jaunes, ou violettes, dont une espèce est le safran à fleur de cette plante. (Famille des iridacées.)

fleur

feuille

bulbe

■ CROCUS

CROIRE v.t. [85] (lat. credere). **1.** Tenir pour vrai, admettre comme réel, certain. Croire une histoire. Je crois ce que vous me dites. **2.** Tenir

Other Books by Évelyne Grossman

In English

The Anguish of Thought (University of Michigan Press, 2017)

In French

La Créativité de la crise (Minuit, 2020)

Éloge de l'hypersensible (Minuit, 2017)

Louise Bourgeois, Three Horizontals, avec F. Danesi et F. Vengeon (Ophrys, Institut National d'Histoire de l'Art, coll. « Voir-Faire-Lire », 2011)

L'Angoisse de penser (Minuit, 2008)

Antonin Artaud, un insurgé du corps (Gallimard, coll. « Découvertes », 2006)

La Défiguration. Artaud, Beckett, Michaux (Minuit, 2004)

Artaud, l'aliéné authentique (Farrago-Léo Scheer, 2003)

La Traversée de la mélancolie (dir. avec N. Piégay) (Séguier, 2002)

Henri Michaux, le corps de la pensée (dir. avec A.-E. Halpern & P. Vilar) (Farrago-Léo Scheer, 2001)

Samuel Beckett: l'écriture et la scène (dir. avec R. Salado) (Sedes, 1998)

L'Esthétique de Beckett (Sedes, 1998)

Artaud / Joyce. Le corps et le texte (Nathan, coll. « Le texte à l'œuvre », 1996)

As Editor

Derniers cahiers d'Ivry, février 1947 – mars 1948 d'Antonin Artaud, édition, notes & préface, 2 vols (Gallimard, 2011)

Cahier d'Ivry, janvier 1948 d'Antonin Artaud, édition & préface (Gallimard, 2006)

Suppôts et suppliciations d'Antonin Artaud, édition, notes & préface (Gallimard, coll. « Poésie / Gallimard », 2006)

50 dessins pour assassiner la magie d'Antonin Artaud, édition, notes & préface (Gallimard, 2004)

Œuvres d'Antonin Artaud, édition, notes & préface (Gallimard, coll. « Quarto », 2004)

Pour en finir avec le jugement de dieu d'Antonin Artaud, édition & préface (Gallimard, coll. « Poésie / Gallimard », 2003)

Van Gogh le suicidé de la société d'Antonin Artaud, édition & préface (Gallimard, coll. « L'imaginaire », 2001)

Évelyne Grossman

The Creativity
of the Crisis

Évelyne Grossman

The Creativity
of the Crisis

Translated by Rainer J. Hanshe

Contra Mundum Press   New York · London · Melbourne

The Creativity of the Crisis
© 2023 Rainer J. Hanshe;
Évelyne Grossman, *La Créativité
de la crise* © 2020 by Les
Éditions de Minuit, 7, rue
Bernard-Palissy, 75006 Paris.

First Contra Mundum Press
edition 2023.

Library of Congress
Cataloguing-in-Publication Data

Grossman, Évelyne, 1952
The Creativity of the Crisis /
Évelyne Grossman

—1st Contra Mundum Press
    Edition

146 pp., 5×8 in.

ISBN 9781940625539

I. Grossman, Évelyne.
II. Title.
III. Hanshe, Rainer J.
IV. Translator.

2023934431

If you want to apply biblio-biographical criteria to me, I confess I wrote my first book quite early, and then nothing for eight years. [...] It's like a hole in my life, a hole of eight years. [...] It's perhaps in these holes that movement takes place. Because the question is how to make a move, how to shatter the wall, to stop banging your head.

Gilles Deleuze, *Negotiations*

Table of Contents

CRISIS OF CREATIVITY

Everyone more or less knows the crisis of inspiration. There is no need to be a sanctioned writer, creator, artist, or inventor since its manifestations are, ironically, within everyone's reach: absence of ideas, sluggish cogitation, numb psyche, overwhelming emptiness. Depressive symptom? Excessive demand toward oneself (perfectionism…)? Severe superego prohibiting too much pleasure? It doesn't really matter since the causes and symptoms are flourishing, in contrast to the nothingness of ideas. The experience can arise regardless of the field in which the inventiveness is exercised, whether it is writing an article, a thesis or an essay, composing a novel, a piece of music, developing a plastic work, writing a film script. Sometimes it is enough to have something to write, a task to complete, even a very modest "paper," a priori without any stake, for the blockage to arise — the breakdown, the turbulence. Keeping our word, meeting deadlines, having something to say… Our time, always quick to imagine new psychic ailments, has conceived this term: "leucosélophobia," blank page syndrome, writing block. If we can doubt that the pathology really exists, we must honor the humorous creativity of the term: *leuco* referring to white, *sélo* to page. Proof that loss of inspiration inspires. It is true that the beauty of certain nothingnesses of thought, as in Mallarmé, do not fail to dazzle: "O nights! nor the deserted light of my lamp / On the empty paper that whiteness defends" ("Sea Breeze," 1865). It should be noted in passing that the Mallarméan reference remains startlingly modern since the idle screen of the digital tool now replacing the blank page does not change the pain of the traversed torments.

When the young Antonin Artaud sends his poems to Jacques Rivière, the editor of the *Nouvelle Revue française*, it's in flamboyant terms that he describes to him this *powerlessness* of thought which suffocates him; not a simple crisis of inspiration, he specifies, but a true déperdition of being: "a central collapse of the soul, a kind of erosion, essential and at the same time fleeting, of thought, [...] the abnormal separation of the elements of thought (the impulse to think, at each of the terminal stratifications of thought, passing through all the states, all the bifurcations, all the localizations of thought and of form)."[1]

Is this what we call in more banal contemporary terms a crisis of creativity? No doubt not. The dark chasms where Artaud sometimes descends are fortunately very far removed from the ordinary torments of creation, those that everyone can one day cross. Faced with the white of inspiration, whether one is an affirmative thinker or a novice student, writer, or artist, the malaise felt is more or less the same; in the face of the crisis a certain democratic parity reigns. The fact remains that the modern crisis of creativity rarely opens up metaphysical abysses. At best, in its benign form, it generates the indispensable surge of adrenaline that permits, the ultimate deadline almost exceeded, one to finally get to work under the pressure of anguish, shame, or guilt. *Deadline* as the Anglo-Saxons say, due date: beyond this limit ... you are *dead* or almost. Should we speak here of a decline in "motivation," to use that catch-all term, somewhat irritating in its consoling flatness, a flatness that tends nowadays to replace the inflexibility of our old moral sanctions: idleness, neglect, sluggishness, lack of will ... or even "lazy bones"? What is motivation? An energy that drives us ... or not. That morale (prohibitive *&* guilt-invoking) tends to be replaced by an energetic force (positive and encouraging) seems to confirm the diagnosis of the sociologist Alain Ehrenberg: "We were entering the modern era of depression: the subject made ill by her conflicts was giving way to the individual paralyzed by her inadequacy."[2] "Motivate" (from the Latin *movere*, to move), is understood here in the proper sense: to take the blocked individual out of his psychic immobility, to shake him, to put him in motion. The modern market can then be opened to various "coaches" and experts, specialists of personal development promising everyone to rediscover "the paths of creativity."

The sociologist Edgar Morin, inventor in 1976 of the term "crisology," readily emphasizes that "crises generate creative forces." The relationship between crisis and creation would then be more complex than it seemed at first glance. Beyond a banal affirmation of the fruitful nature of crises, in the systemic thought of Morin, the crisis involves both disorganization and reorganization: "Any increased disorganization effectively carries with it the risk of death, but also the luck of a new reorganization, of a creation, of a going beyond. As McLuhan said, *breakdown is a potential breakthrough.*"[3] This is to say once again that breakdown [*l'effondrement*] can lead to many creative breakthroughs [*des percées créatrices*]. However, let us not hasten to see in it a new avatar of the notion of "creative destruction" defended by the economist Joseph Schumpeter.[4] Morin's analysis, joined by many other thinkers, rather opens onto another type of observation, that of a current crisis engendered by the loss of faith in a progress supposed to bring wellbeing to the whole of humanity in accordance with the ideal of the European philosophy of the Enlightenment. We have long believed, he emphasizes, that science, technology, economics could solve the world's great problems. However, despite the undeniable benefits, the alleged "side effects" are in fact cataclysmic and the potential "collateral victims" are counted in the millions. In this model, the crisis is first a sign of disillusionment with the promise of an unlimited progressive development. It does not work or it no longer works; the engine has stalled, skepticism arises about the promised opening of a bright future. The depressed ritornello: "it was better before!" signals the collapse of our hopes in the future. Nostalgia for the past then conceals a painful complaint: I no longer have a future; before me, there is nothing (*no future*, as the *punks* used to say, in the last century). Depression, Freud suggests, is a disease of time.

It is possible that this famous ideal of limitless progress is not foreign to the infantile dream that psychoanalysis calls the "fantasy of all-powerfulness." To believe that there is no limit to the forward march of progress, no border to human power, would then be akin to a fantasy of immortality, a refusal of human finitude.[5] Many are indeed the psychoanalysts who, after Freud, have evoked the archaic spaces of a symbiotic mother-child sphere, the first state of indifferentiation, of omnipotent fusion with the mother, in which the "I" is not differentiated yet from the "non-I," where the inside and the outside only gradually come to be perceived as different.[6] From this limitless maternal body-world, the very young child (the *infans*: the one who does not yet speak) must separate, in other words lose it, to be. At the frontiers of this loss, the first formative crisis is developed, which Melanie Klein calls the "depressive position": separation, with the mother recognized as having a life of her own, the mother-object with finite limits.[7] What Klein calls the maternal body, let us remember, is not necessarily that of a mother but of anyone who fulfills the maternal function of nourishment and protection against intrusion and the anguish of death. This first crisis is therefore essential for accessing the human symbolic order in the sense of being part of a Law that limits but also relieves (everything is not possible, I am not all-powerful). The fantasy of omnipotence can however resurface in certain poetico-psychotic universes such as those of Artaud. If his *Theater of Cruelty* wants to "challenge man organically," to remake the human body, it is because it intends to give back to man the immortality of unfathomable spaces: "This leads us to reject man's usual limitations and powers and infinitely extends the frontiers of what we call reality."[8]

Creativity, in the psychoanalytic sense that I am questioning here, is understood in a much broader way than artistic activity in the strict sense. It refers to the power of creation specific to the human psyche: imaginary representations, fantasies, dreams and daydreams, hallucinations, to say nothing of those failing-successful creations that are lapses or lost acts. Some, like D.W. Winnicott, go so far as to evoke a "creative drive" in the universal sense of the vital drive which, confronted with the "immense shock represented by the loss of omnipotence" that the individual must face at the very beginning of his life, allows the creation of the first "subjective object" that the baby creates. Ancestor of future transitional objects, this "subjective object," a paradox of psychic creation, is "the first 'not-me' possession" in the intermediate area of experience, between inner reality and external life.[9] Fundamentally then, for psychoanalysis, psychic creativity is anchored in the elaboration of lack and loss. It is also in this sense that Pierre Fédida proposes to differentiate the *depressed state* (or depression) and *depressivity* (or depressive capacity). In the *depressed state*, the temporalities specific to psychic life (remembering, representing, desiring, projecting) seem frozen in the stillness of the body. It is an experience of dead life, of life that has become inanimate. Contrarily, the depressive capacity is the ability to maintain a living and creative link between loss, mourning, absence, lack — those often painful trials and negative experiences that all subjects are called to undergo — and creativity. In other words, the depressed state is a stasis, a failure of the depressive capacity, and the role of the therapist is precisely to "re-animate this inanimate psychic being," to restore to the depressed patient his depressive capacity.[10] The interest of this conception, which is in line with Klein and Winnicott, is to emphasize that the opposition between death and life is uncertain and complex. Likewise, the crisis of creativity should not be understood as a simply radical opposition between fertility & sterility. Reintegrated into the vitality of a pulsional dynamic, it assumes the free play of articulations between unbinding forces (death, emptiness) and binding forces (life, desire). We cannot therefore simply oppose the crisis and its resolution, creation and destruction. All creation originates in the complexity of the erotic process, in the Freudian sense of the term: it puts desire and its powerlessness into play. It is also what Roland Barthes, another great theorist of desire and creation, knew.

Barthes wanted all his life to become a writer but never succeeded. He knew perfectly well that a literary critic or a literary theorist is hardly the equivalent of a true writer, in the noble or classical sense of the term, like Chateaubriand or Tolstoy, two of his models. For a long time he sought to demonstrate with brio that between the two practices of critical reading and novelistic writing the difference was only of degree. All true reading, he repeated, is secretly inscribed in an imaginary register, that of the desire to write; moreover, it is an interpretative creation. His last two courses at the Collège de France are entitled *The Preparation of the Novel*. He questions with a slight irony what it means to "prepare" to write a novel, even "to prepare" a novel. Do you prepare a novel the way you prepare a meal? Is there a recipe you can just follow, or any trade secrets? Often, he notes, the "preparation" is not very appetizing, which is why cooks chase curious people out of the kitchen. The "preparation" in the kitchen is usually unrelated to "the excellence of the dish that arrives pompously on the table." Supreme elegance (a shame to conceal?), the work of creation, must not be seen in the accomplished work, even if everyone knows perfectly well that "a 'preparation' is actually composed of repetitions, reversals, uncertainties, mistakes…"[11] Thus Flaubert, writing to his niece about the composition of *Bouvard and Pécuchet*: "I flounder, I cross out, I despair, etc."

Writers are sometimes questioned about their writing rites and rhythms, pretending to believe in some magical practice necessary for their inspiration: what quill, pen, pencil, or type of computer, what form of paper, what auspicious time of day or night, what posture (standing like Hemingway and Artaud?), what fetishes … distant heirs to the fertility stones and other fertility rituals to which sterile couples once submitted? We readily cite the famous dressing gown that Balzac liked to wear and whose drapery Rodin immortalized in his sculpture, *Monument to Balzac*. To say nothing of the thirty or so coffees the same Balzac was supposed to drink every day to stimulate his imagination. Among many writers and thinkers, other sometimes illicit adjuvants are mentioned in a low voice, no doubt so as not to reduce the supposed omnipotence of creativity to an all too human insufficiency: absinthe, chloral hydrate, opium, cocaine, amphetamines...

Without it being necessary to mention a particular alcoholic or cocaine addict writer, what reader indeed would identify with a needy or faint-hearted writer? Gide, who was said to be going through a depressive phase at the time, painted a cleverly cruel portrait of this type of writer in his short novel, *Marshlands*.[12] The narrator, a literary man whose name is unknown, spends his days engaged in petty worldly occupations & writing a book about little or nothing. While others act (his friend Hubert "is a member of four industrial companies; he and his brother-in-law run another hail insurance company ..."), what does he do? "I write *Marshlands*," he invariably replies to anyone who questions him. Its hero is called Tityre, in homage to a character of Virgil because, he says, "I do not know how to invent." Tityre? A wise man or an idler who is content with what he has and who takes care of little: looking at the swamps, killing a few teals to eat them. The material of the book? Precisely that. To a friend's question: "Why do you write?" (a famous question sometimes asked in literary reviews), the narrator replies with disconcerting candor: "Me? — I don't know, — probably to have something to do." To the same question, Samuel Beckett replied, "Good for nothing else."

In *The Preparation of the Novel*, Barthes therefore questions the literary myth of "the fertile crisis." He spotted in the once famous textbook of literature for high school classes, the *Castex and Surer* ("at the same time perfectly mythological and well done"), what he called a real *tic*: "The life of almost all writers is articulated by a central *crisis* (even if it is not situated in the middle of life), a crisis from which a renewal of works stems, that is to say from which the triumphant Work leaves, regenerated." He likes to enumerate a typology of the various creative crises identified over the pages of the manual: "anecdotal" crises (remarriage of Baudelaire's mother, decisive trips by Stendhal or Gide), "passionate or sentimental" crises (Lamartine, Musset, Apollinaire), "political" crises (exiles of Mme de Staël or Victor Hugo), "spiritual" crises (Chateaubriand, Renan)… This romantic myth of the fertile crisis, he remarks, generates not only its heroes but also its rejects: "The rare biographies where [this crisis] does not exist seem quite pathetic: disinherited and lost authors, who do not even know how to enact a creative crisis: they are not heroes of literature since they are not martyrs of Childbirth, of Drama." [13]

Following Barthes, we could identify a modern rewriting of this myth of the fruitful crisis — the resilience trend — in the link frequently woven between trauma and creation. [14] An interesting issue of the online journal *Apparatus* recently explored the hypothesis that

trauma (etymologically: "the wound") could consti-
tute an extreme experience that could shed light on
the process of creation. A series of articles thus invites
us to question the great traumas, real or imaginary,
of Western literature (Montaigne's fall from a horse,
Rousseau's accident with a dog, Marcel's near-fainting
at Guermantes…), but also the post-traumatic works of
certain painters such as those of Sam Francis or Joseph
Beuys after a plane crash, or of the French painter Germain Roesz, following a long coma.[15]

The philosopher Jean-Louis Déotte thus dialogues
with Roesz, a former butcher's apprentice at the slaugh-
terhouses of Colmar in Alsace, who returned to life,
still a young adult, coming out of a long coma caused
by a road accident that should have been his death:
"The origin of my painting lies in a founding shock, a
comatic trauma. Not to see or think about the world.
To know, upon returning, among the living and the
spoken word, that part of oneself, of one's conscience,
was abolished, forgotten."[16] More than once, over
the course of these meetings and analyses, the fantasy
emerges of a fundamental wound reinvested not only
as a foundation but also as a matrix of the work. Thus,
an imaginary is constructed that we could call: "the fertilization of the artist by nothingness." It is indeed this
fracturing event, as specialists of psycho-trauma say, that
allows the opening, at the end of a dazzling illumina-
tion or of a long coma, of a world outside the natural

or simply human order: the myth of fertilization that rekindles the great theological myths of the creation of the world, the work passing in a mysterious and overwhelming way from non-being to being, from nothingness to existence.

We find this pattern in Pierre Guyotat, a contemporary writer, a great explorer of the non-human limits of creation, familiar with journeys to the vicinity of death. In a short and dense récit, *Coma*, Guyotat recounts his "great crisis" of the spring of 1982 that had led him, from progressive decline to comatose fainting, "to the verge of death." Throughout the book, he retraces the dismemberment, the shattering, of his body and his slow awakening between horror and happiness. In Guyotat, effraction mixes the sexual with the theological; it is in that transgressive mode that he literally tears from the hole in his flesh a work in which the creation of language and of the world is tirelessly remade. Thus, for example, echoing a young admirer declaring to him: "you have freed the imagination" (you said: "liberated"?), he pursues his eternal quest: "With whom to share carnally — derisory compared to this is that, as a Christian child, I imagine for my life: being rendered by lions, disembowelment by a bull, struck by the thunderbolt of God; then adolescent, ravaged by brothels! —, on the spot, to dissolve its fixity, this 'happiness,' this beginning of the accomplishment of a destiny that I wanted, in the very quarter of the city where I confronted it with a reality outside myself." [17] Heartbreak, wound where the end of the world and the coming into the world are endlessly replayed.

We can also imagine transfiguring the creative wound into a quasi-concept, a vital event raised to the level of moral philosophy. This is where Gilles Deleuze succeeds with brio when he evokes as a "pure event" the war wound that left the young poet Joë Bousquet permanently crippled. Seriously injured by a bullet in the spine in 1918 at the age of 21, he spent the rest of his days paralyzed, bedridden in his room in Carcassonne where he continued his work as a writer until his death in 1950. There he wrote a number of poetic and often tormented texts, sometimes with philosophical or spiritual aims. Deleuze devotes magnificent pages to a portrait of Bousquet as a Stoic philosopher. "We sometimes hesitate," he writes, "to call a concrete or poetic way of life Stoic, as if the name of a doctrine were too bookish, too abstract to designate the most personal connection with a wound. But where do the doctrines come from if not from wounds and vital aphorisms, which are so many speculative anecdotes with their charge of exemplary provocation? We must call Joë Bousquet a Stoic." [18] He then quotes Bousquet's sentence, which will now symbolize in itself for many readers the grand figure of the poet of Carcassonne:

"My wound existed before me, I was born to embody it."[19] Bousquet is exemplary in the eyes of Deleuze of this admirable moral standing that we should imitate without complaining or taking ourselves for martyrs (two forms of the same *ressentiment*). "Either morality makes no sense," Deleuze sums up, "or else that's what it means, it has nothing else to say: not to be unworthy of what happens to us. On the contrary, grasping what is happening as unfair and undeserved (it's always someone's fault) is what makes our wounds loathsome, *ressentiment* itself, *ressentiment* against the event."[20]

Deleuze's analysis is beautiful, incontestable. He knowingly ignores the complaint and discouragement, sometimes self-loathing, of someone who says he is "crushed under the weight of [his] frozen, useless body"[21] and who often fought against pain with the help of morphine, cocaine, or opium. It also leaves in the shadow another aspect of Bousquet's writing, infinitely more troubling — that of the man obsessed with women and the feverish love he has for them, inseparable for him from creation. He maintained an abundant literary correspondence with writers, artists, and intellectuals, such as the philosopher Simone Weil, but also many young women whom he attracted around his crippled body. He sends them loving, luminous, and sensitive letters in which he often passes from disgust at his infirmity to the radiant exaltation it inspires in him; he then feels enhaloed by a sacred wound in which he will be able, as he says, to "incorporate" his vocation — a Christ posture if ever there was one. He wrote to one woman: "Is it excessive to pretend to assign to my wound the somewhat special character that a sacrament confers upon certain men?"[22] Make no mistake about it though: it is not about exercising an ascetic priesthood through writing but to enjoy the desiring body that writing gives back to him.

Bousquet had in effect a revelation: his wounded flesh literally remained pierced with a desire that remained intact: "deprived of all my virile strength, I had kept my desire intact in my ruined body. I remember the astonishment I felt when my wounds had barely healed. The same love for women lived in my inert body."[23] A consuming desire thus survives this presumed dead body and its wound becomes the living center of his writing from the day he understands that it is precisely "this insufficiency that is creative."[24] This is what he will repeat throughout his life as a writer to his many interlocutors when they evoked the genesis of his work, between mystical inspiration and more carnally earthly conception. The famous *Cahier noir*, long kept secret and published thirty-nine years after his death, is also proof. Throughout the book, amorous exaltation meets the tireless repetition of the same perverse scene repeated in infinite variations; he incarnates all the roles there — father, daughter, child, woman — in an erotic whirlwind wherein he never ceases to explore the hole in the body to be opened in order to enter by force and ecstatically be reborn from it: "In the clear water of her attitude it seemed to me that all the depth of a sky that was in me was barely falling asleep again by the wind of the full daylight. Separating with my two hands the cheeks, which had been modestly congealed by her fatness, I revealed for the first time the shadowy slit [...]. I pushed myself violently into her nakedness, stuck my eye so to speak into the keyhole [...]. This is how when we sodomize the one we love, we penetrate into her with all the matter of which we are built."[25] In more encrypted terms, he already described in *Traduit du Silence* the embraces in which his body of poetic flesh was created through the love of women: "I only really felt connected to the one who, in order to better surrender herself, turned her back on herself, and agreed to bring out, so to speak, the woman of the embrace that united us. She agreed to bind me within her only to an image of my own body, the body of a man. [...] This love that I will have for her will be sodomic love and I am delighted. [...] He who sodomizes a woman unites only with himself."[26] In other words, the paths of poetic creation are impenetrable to those who refuse to engage with them as a body.

Bousquet's heroism? No doubt as well, but between desire and stoic acquiescence, there is a difference: desire makes you write; morality — even stoic —, that's less certain.

It has therefore become difficult for us to completely believe in a model linking trauma and creation in the elementary form of the fruitful crisis, like *Castex and Surer*. Every great work, we suspect, does not necessarily have to pay with a symbolic traversal of death, following the old linear and Christlike scheme: "death — resurrection." Samuel Beckett ironically mocked it in advance, he who recalled being born on Good Friday, the day of Christ's death; if you are hoping for resurrection, you can go to hell![27] And yet, where does the recurrence of these modern, tenacious, although more discreet variants of the pangs and collapses that once characterized the creative crisis, come from? Certainly, like the great hysterical attacks, the crisis seems to have weakened, civilized. Something, however, still strikes us in its alternating rhythm of exaltation and discouragement, its enigmatic pain.

Let's try to enter into those kitchens of creation that Barthes spoke of. Let us reread, for example, what is described by a writer apparently closer to us, ordinary people, Louis Calaferte, who died in 1994, a novelist who is sometimes a little forgotten but who is nevertheless the author of more than 50 books, récits, short stories, poetry, plays, not to mention his abundant notebooks. His extraordinary first novel, *Requiem des innocents*, published in 1952, recounted the apocalypse of post-war life in the suburbs, just before the construction of the modern H.L.M.: the "zone," the mud of the wasteland, misery, alcohol, violence, children left to fend for themselves.[28] His third novel, *Septentrion*, published in 1963, also largely autobiographical, describes his journey toward writing marked by the regular alternation of quasi-hallucinatory periods of inspiration & depressive episodes where he thinks of abandoning everything. Thus, jubilantly, what he calls the territories "of the fusion of life into life" open up within writing: "How to explain what goes on in the chest during those sudden bursts of detonation that regulate the beating of your arteries to the secret rhythms of the world? The sensation of becoming for good the hyper-receptive center of the universe in gestation. Thought brilliantly exits the seat of captivity. Solves, understands, elucidates with astonishing sharpness."[29] Shortly after, however, succeeding the creative impetus, and as if by punitive backlash, the dizzying fallout began:

> The creative eruption that had swept over me during the day would end in flames. A heavy void suddenly replaced it. No trace of momentum. The soul since dried up. Each time I felt the disgust rise; the sadness of an impotence that I was no match for. The old ghost of failing still lurking in the shadows, threatening.

Why at that time was I not able to get out
of that inner apathy that acts on the mind
like an anesthetic? Years of leading the fight,
brushing against the bottom of something
that must have felt like the last seconds of resistance before the agony. Between the will
to live and the obligation to die. Fall full of
abandonment. To scrap the ambition to ex-
press oneself. Renounce. Recognize oneself
as nothing & thus try to live in peace.[30]

In these pitiless alternations (or pitiful, as one likes),
Freud would undoubtedly identify a classic neurotic
conflict between pleasure and the forbidden: orgias-
tic fusion via the ecstasy of writing; sexual breakdown,
impotence, via its depressive side. The too strong erot-
icization of creation then strikes it with a prohibition,
the libido transforms into anxiety, for reasons obviously
specific to each one. The ecstatic orgasm is followed
by punishment in the form of guilt, sadness, feelings
of helplessness, self-annihilation. How then to fight
against the ferocity of such a prohibiting superego if
not by an exhausting expenditure of energy, skillful
development of avoidance maneuvers, preventive
stratagems, endless rationalizations with an absolutist
aim (what I am writing is nothing, anyway, let's go
without fear ...)?

There are many who know, to varying degrees, such a punitive ... *&* castrating scheme, Freud would always say. How to exit such a vicious circle, except via masochist complacency, the morbid ecstasy of rehashing one's own inadequacy? We understand the temptation of Calaferte: it is better to abstain from all writing rather than this exhausting pendulum. And yet ...

Calaferte is not the only one to describe with acuity these painful oscillations between creative plenitude and impotent emptiness. On a completely different level of the social scale, Jean-René Huguenin, a pampered child of the beautiful Parisian districts,[31] barely a few years younger than Calaferte: he also attests to a less detached and easy writing experience one might have believed from such a gifted young man, a precocious writer hailed by critics from his first novel, extolled by François Mauriac and Louis Aragon. *La Côte sauvage* [The Wild Coast], published by Le Seuil in 1960, was immediately successful. He immediately set about a second novel that never saw the light of day: two years later, at the age of 26, he died tragically on a road near Rambouillet behind the wheel of the car he was driving. From Huguenin, there remains this novel, *La Côte sauvage*, a few literary articles, and the *Journal* in which he chronicled his social and amorous life while reporting daily on the difficult progress of the writing of his novel.

As with Calaferte, although very differently, periods of crisis or doubt follow moments of great fertility. Thus on May 4, 1961: "There are days when my brain stops, exactly like a watch, and I remain broken down whole afternoons, unable to work, to imagine, to read, and even to think." [32] Contrarily, on other days, he describes the prodigious progress of his writing (articles for magazines, editing his novel) at the cost of a frenzied work pace to which he constrains himself with an iron will until exhaustion. For example, on February 5, 1960: "It is 1 A.M. Since 10:30 in the morning, I haven't stopped. [...] But it is time, constancy, fidelity, tenacity, continuity that count. [...] It's about advancing, forcing, going beyond measure, and that's it." Or again, 10 days later: "The challenge of the 60 hours is taken up, the bet held, I am in order. It's 2 A.M., I've been working 12 hours straight today (the whole first scene of the 6th chapter, well done, I think, now). You have to maintain this order, this demand, this harshness toward yourself, until it becomes perfectly natural." [33]

With Huguenin, we have apparently returned to traditional bourgeois and Catholic morality: harsh demands, self-control, over-perseverance of one's own weaknesses. At that price, the work can be written. It is not far from being a punishment itself, asceticism cutting off its author from an easier life. The writer is a monk ... who would have become fruitful. Incidentally, who will speak of the phantasmal weight of the doctor fathers with creators like Huguenin, Bousquet, even Proust or Foucault... The latter was not far from fantasizing about the scalpel of his father as a weapon with which he would one day rummage inside him.[34]

Let us compare for a moment these two modes of the creative crisis, in Calaferte and Huguenin. In the first case: creative climax and guilt, threat of sterility, this "castration of being" as said Artaud. In the second, a severe ideal of greatness and of self-mastery, the writing of which — it's the discovery of this psychic organization — can complement itself: "Definitely, I hate weakness and the weak," writes Huguenin. "I hate fear, moderation, reserve. The blow of despair will no longer hold. Tonight, deep forces suddenly erupt. [...] During these last months, I have been pathetic, contenting myself with feelings already experienced, with work without depth."[35] We can thus detect in Huguenin the imperious requirement of a morality that accepts the ecstasy of writing only if it is denied, excused in advance and as if covered by the glorious asceticism of manly training and deprivation (of alcohol, of going out, of an easy love life): firm moral ideal of a social class that experienced an exodus on the roads like a humiliation and which still blushes at the defeat of the French army in 1940. Huguenin often returns there. The lack of inspiration, after all? A defeatism, peculiar to the corruption of the era, an absence of will unworthy of a real man. A week before his death, he wrote: "The modern crisis — which I too am suffering from right now: lack of will → lack of action → ennui → self-hatred → lack of will, etc."[36]

In the end, unsurprisingly, we find in Calaferte the same martial ideal, the same reference to self-sacrifice. He too evokes "the inexpressible sum of cruel tenacity, ruthless toward oneself, involved in this tour de force of becoming a creator," this "final surpassing of oneself."[37] Writing is a struggle. And besides, Calaferte sanctimoniously wonders: "I would have liked to know if the men whose talent I admired, painters or writers, had suffered the same fits of depression." He forgets the women in passing, few in number it is true at the time, with some notable exceptions, who engage in writing and see themselves recognized. Huguenin adds: the work is torn off in battle, victory over oneself must be conquered relentlessly: "I have been going back a year — intolerable idea! Everything I write is bad [...]. I live without appetite, without taste, nothing inspires me. Even my love for Marianne [his fiancée] is at this moment a weak love, the refuge of a coward."[38] Writing is a heroism. So be it.

Does this mean that only a hero is capable of engendering a work? Let us not hasten to identify too quickly the "masculinist" reproduction of gender stereotypes. Rather, it could be that the crisis of creativity signals the failure of the exhausting and endless attempt to embody all the roles in the great sex scene of child-birth (papa, mama, and child). At times, the plasticity of identifications becomes tense, the machine seizes up and the creator pitifully replays in the alternation of his postures the same hesitation between masculine and feminine as the great hysterics of Freud: sometimes the vigor of the inspired impulse, sometimes abandonment or nervous withdrawal.[39]

Even when it functions apparently without a hitch, the beautiful mechanics of virile power, not to say spermatic, of man-writing, such as some ruminate on the fantasy of it, also hides neurotic springs more complex than one likes to imagine. I will take just one example, that of Georges Simenon (Calaferte alludes to it in *Septentrion*), a flamboyant representative of an astonishing libidinal energy that accumulated books, money, women, luxury cars, various homes (33, it seems). Prolific, unstoppable Simenon, both as writer (400 novels, half of which are under a pseudonym) and as lover; at 74 years old, he counts his sexual antics: 10,000 women, he claims, including 8,000 "professionals." Between 1931 & 1974, he published an average of five novels per year. He writes in the morning, at the machine, from scribbled notes. He can thus complete a novel in just over a week. The man, however, is anything but serene:

a great worrier, it seems, who read Freud, Adler, and Jung from a very young age. His insatiable frenzy of writing, far from simply raising a joyful creative vitality, would have had, according to some, an anxiolytic function. Simenon is the man with inkblood, as his biographer Pierre Assouline aptly remarks.[40]

It is therefore clear that any question relating to creativity easily engenders tension or inhibition, in both men and women. If creation is so desirable and gives rise to such conflicts, perhaps there is a massive and often denied link between procreation and creation. In any case, this is the hypothesis that allows us to explore two women, creators of particularly fruitful theories, the psychoanalyst Melanie Klein and the anthropologist Françoise Héritier.

All her life, Melanie Klein explored the in effect instinctual violence at work in the newborn, the violent archaic conflicts that he must go through in order to develop and create his own psychic autonomy. Klein describes the attacks on the "breast," this primordial life-giving figure, evoking the opposition that Saint Augustine also saw between a creative force, Life, and a destructive force, Envy. "The good breast that nourishes and initiates the loving relationship with the mother is representative of the life drive; it is also felt to be the first manifestation of creativity," she writes. It is this same archaic representation of a primitive, creative, and all-powerful breast that arouses in the newborn a destructive envy as violent as it is unconscious. What is envy, compared to jealousy or oral greed? Klein defines it as "the angry feeling that another person possesses and enjoys something desirable — the envious impulse being to take it away or spoil it." The capacity to give and to preserve life being seen as the most precious gift, "creativity becomes the deepest cause for envy."[41] Over weeks and months, a gradual pacification takes place & an identification with the creative breast, this first good internalized object, is put in place. This identification is what gives the original impetus to human creativity. Between devastating violence and loving identification then emerges the difficult psychic journey that the little human being must accomplish. Let a disturbance arise at the heart of this delicate balance and it is the development of that first creative capacity that is affected. "My analytical experience," Klein points out, "has taught me that envious feelings about creativity play a fundamental role in any disruption of the creative process."[42]

If Freud & especially Lacan could be reproached for sometimes forgetting the mother, the opposite reproach was addressed to Klein. Faced with this apparently hypostasized breast, the first principle generating all the capacities to be created, we have sometimes wondered where the father is in Klein & many Kleinian works.

Throughout their theory, in spite of their denials, the mother, the "femininity of the mother," the "maternal breast" ... The fundamental unconscious model is the creativity of the Mother, repeats the Anglo-Saxon line of Kleinian psychoanalysts. Rather, it is that of the Father, resume Freud and the theologians (the almighty creative Father). Should we then imagine a "breast" that would be potentially *also* paternal, outside narrow physiological representation, or prior to any sexual partition? Psychoanalysis, long stuck in its binary and hierarchical sexual representations (see Freud's *Three Essays on Sexual Theory* in 1905), is now attentive to these questions.

A comparable question is at the heart of the work of Françoise Héritier, a great figure of French anthropology. Successor of Claude Lévi-Strauss at the Collège de France where she held the Chair of Comparative Study of African Societies, she worked to question the famous structural model of the exchange of women, the "theory of alliance" in formerly "primitive" societies, exhibited for the first time by Lévi-Strauss in *Elementary Structures of Parenthood* in 1949. One presupposition of that theory remains unquestioned, she emphasizes: why do men feel they have the right to use women as a figure of exchange? What she demonstrates can be summed up succinctly as follows: it is on the perception of the difference of bodies *&* the different role of the sexes in reproduction that humanity has supported the fundamental binary category of its thought: identical *vs.* different. Social organization is built on that first biological model of opposition. Yet, in moving from the biological to the social, the pairs of opposites become hierarchical; the distinction between female and male is universal, but nowhere is this binary opposition symmetrical. Any thought of difference thus fits into a classification in which the masculine pole is always and everywhere valued, assigned a positive sign.[43] Héritier gives many illustrations, for example this one: "The ethnological observation shows us that the positive is always on the masculine side, and the negative on the feminine side. It does not depend on the category itself: the same qualities are not valued in the same way in all latitudes. No, it depends on whether it is male or female. [...] For example, with us, in the West, 'active' [...] is valued, and therefore associated with the masculine, while 'passive,' less appreciated, is associated with the feminine. In India, it is the opposite: passivity is the sign of serenity [...]. Passivity here is masculine and it is valued, activity — seen as always a bit messy — is feminine and it is devalued."[44]

This recurring fact according to which the masculine has everywhere been considered to be worth more than the feminine Héritier attributes fundamentally to what she calls, in almost Kleinian terms, the masculine *envy* of the fertility of women. Indeed, she points out, "women reproduce identically [they make daughters] but they also have the exorbitant capacity to produce bodies different from themselves [those of their sons]." Even more: "To reproduce identically, a man *has to pass through a female body*. He cannot do it on his own. It is this incapacity that establishes the fate of female humanity."[45] According to the anthropologist, then, we understand this millennial obsession of men to appropriate and control the power of fertility, this power of creation of women.

The demonstrations of Héritier, like those of Klein, as different as they may be, can undoubtedly be debated as to the dominant role they give to the maternal or to the feminine. In my eyes, this is fundamental: they both had the merit of emphasizing certain blind spots in the strong (male) theories that preceded them; even more, the explanatory power of their own work as to the ignored or denied genesis of the great theories of creation is indisputable. From the point of view that interests me here, that of the crisis of creativity, they allow us to better understand the difficult genesis of any creative process, its consubstantial fragility, if we conceive of it in exclusive terms of bringing a work into the world. In other words, if we rhyme creation and procreation.

Here again, the bringing to light of unconscious processes by that mad creator Artaud is enlightening. If it is true that, unlike the neurotic where it is repressed, the unconscious in the psychotic manifests itself in the open, then Artaud brilliantly reveals the erotic-procreative genesis of the creative process for some writers. To think, for him, is first of all to give thought a body, to incarnate it in a form, a text. Yet, repeatedly, either his thought fails to be born and aborts, or it solidifies in the body-shackle of a dead language. This is the recurring complaint of all his early texts. What fails every time is the embodiment of the idea, and his thought "de-corporates," it fails to take shape, it aborts. Thinking *is conceivable* and from there all the rest follows: the bringing into the world of the idea fails and that failure repeats, mimicking it, the failing [*ratage*] of all birth in a living body (any procreated body, for him, is doomed to death). It is not that there is strictly speaking a prohibition to think but there is a prohibition to *conceive* in him a thought that is his own. What is missing is the moment of the subjectification of thought, its elaboration in the matrix of the mind, its birth in my language: "As soon as the slightest intellectual will intervenes in order to allow an image or an idea to take body by taking form, [...] the disease manifests its presence, its continuity, one would say that it is enough for the mind to have wanted to enjoy an idea or interior image for this creative climax to be taken away, the spoken image regularly aborts ..."[46] If thought aborts, it is because its individuation, its voluntary and concerted birthing, like *my* thought, reproduces *in me* the violence of this birth rushed into death by giving birth to me. Everything happens as if, by identifying the mother's deadly power for him, he could in turn conceive of a production of his mind only on the model of abortion and of 'scraping': "what you took for my works was only the waste of myself, those scrapings of the soul that the normal man does not welcome."[47]

What can we deduce at this stage? First, it is hardly surprising that many writers have sought to extricate themselves from that infernal "creation / procreation" pair. This is demonstrated by the attempts that some people make to imagine a neutral or impersonal (or even non-human) creation subject. Moreover, we must resist the seduction of an insufficiently analyzed union between "crisis" and "creation," otherwise the terms will be exchanged in a perpetual and exhausting tourniquet: crisis of creativity, creativity of crisis.

In a short article first published in Italian in 1969 in *Il Corriere della Sera*, Roland Barthes enumerated "Ten Reasons to Write." Once the reputedly futile reasons have been eliminated (satisfying your friends, irritating your enemies, producing something new, the ecstatic experience, feeling different...), one of the reasons mentioned makes it possible to slightly shift the focus of the question. When asked "why write?," Barthes replied: "Because writing decenters the word, the individual, the person, accomplishes a work whose origin is indistinguishable."[48] Beyond the theme of the time (the decentering of the subject), I hear a motive that for me is essential: because you never really know *who* is writing; not who am I, I who write, but *what*, inside or outside of me, writes? A dizzying question, bordering on madness, which Samuel Beckett, among others, will take up.

THE IMPERSONAL AS A CREATOR

It is hard to imagine a Surrealist poet short of inspiration. The technique of automatic writing can indeed pass for the antidote par excellence to any neurotic guilt: words, under the "dictation of thought," as André Breton says, are written all alone or almost.[49] Images spring, inexhaustible, from a "subliminal" world (not very Freudian after all)[50] that opens access to an apparently inexhaustible source of creativity, without crisis or painful interruption.

In his *First Surrealist Manifesto* of 1924, Breton offered some advice to those who would like to try the experiment: "Forget about your genius, your talents, & the talents of everyone else. [...] Write quickly, without any preconceived subject, fast enough so that you will not remember what you're writing & be tempted to read what you have written. The first sentence will come all on its own, so true is it that every second there is a sentence unknown to our conscious thought which only asks to be externalized. [...] Continue as much as you want. Rely on the inexhaustible nature of the murmur."[51] The watchword of automatic writing is twin: liberation of the creative energy peculiar to language, end of belief in the solitary genius, master of his word.

The phrase of Lautréamont is taken up with enthusiasm: "Poetry must be made by everyone. Not by one." By everyone? *Orgy*, Artaud hears disdainfully, always quick to send writing back to its organic *&* sexual model. So make way for collective manifestœs, fruitful fortuitous encounters, fertile short-circuits of images, the emergence of words in freedom escaping the control of one who can no longer say he is the sole author.

In 1919, André Breton *&* Philippe Soupault had written *The Magnetic Fields* together. Breton in his first *Manifesto* stresses the poetic power that Soupault and himself then brought to light, afterwards discovering in their pages "the illusion of an extraordinary verve, a great deal of emotion, a considerable choice of images of a quality such that we would not have been capable of preparing a single one in longhand..." A distant reference or not to the Platonic theory of poetic delirium (ecstasy and unreason), even to Epicurean physics (deviated fall of colliding atoms, birth of matter), the practice of the automatic writing of *Magnetic Fields* reveals a psychic universe that has become a force field, carried away by the speed of particles in perpetual vibration. "It goes forward, borne by these images that enrapture it, which scarcely leave it any time to breathe upon the fire in its fingers."[52] However, if automatic writing can thus flow freely, it is not without danger for those who practice it. Later in his *Interviews* Breton will stress that the automatism practiced in *The Magnetic Fields*, written for the most part in eight days of daily practice, sometimes for eight or ten consecutive hours, also proved to be violently destructive: "We could not, despite everything, do more. And hallucinations lurked. A few more chapters, written at v"""" speed (much greater than v") & I probably wouldn't be, now, looking at this edition."[53]

We can better understand here the interest that Maurice Blanchot showed in the Surrealist enterprise. What automatic writing had brought to light was, according to him, "this infinite murmur opened near us, underneath our common utterances, which seem like an inexhaustible source." As Blanchot analyzes with acuity, the failures of automatic writing will never discourage Breton, even though the misunderstanding was inherent in an enterprise that seemed to offer an "easy method" that was always effective, exalting this myth of a poetry "made close to everyone" and through which anyone could become a poet immediately. Yet, he insists, the enterprise was risky and he salutes their courage in approaching what he calls the "whispering immensity" of "the errant word."[54] According to Blanchot, the work indeed requires that the writer lose all individual character and that he become "the empty place where impersonal affirmation is announced." What is meant here by "impersonal"? First, at a minimum, this: do not take yourself for a creative subject.

And Blanchot does not have enough ferocious words to castigate writers who imagine they have a message: "they have something to say, a world within themselves to liberate, a mandate to assume, their unjustifiable life to justify."[55] In terms closer to the assumed project of the Surrealists, the creative force of words once liberated, it is the artist's entire rational and individual subjectivity that is shattered.

The crisis has therefore shifted: no longer that of creativity but that which, voluntarily and knowingly fomented, dethrones the creative subject in favor of an irrational and sometimes terrifying outburst of words and images.

I open here a parenthesis. In a more radical sense and undoubtedly foreign to Surrealism, the impersonal according to Blanchot requires rising to the height of sacrifice. One writes, as he phrases it, only by letting go of oneself: "The work demands of the writer that he lose all 'nature,' all character, and ceasing to relate to others & to himself by the decision that makes him an 'I,' he becomes the empty place where impersonal affirmation is announced."[56] Far from any narcissistic reassurance, writing advances through an interlacing of contradictory forces that always threaten to undo it. Blanchot calls this tireless process "*désoeuvrement*" (the unworking): not inaction, the absence of work, impotence in Calaferte or the arrested brain of Huguenin (simply negative movement), but a force of destruction that animates the work, an unstable movement that gnaws at it and that must be endured. It's the very movement of creation according to Blanchot and we must persevere in the strange energy of *désoeuvrement* "by enduring the distress of an irremediable failure" until the blaze of color, as in van Gogh. Or even the dazzling Surrealist images, one might add. What the Surrealists had therefore discovered was not the promise of a creativity that was within everyone's reach but the existence of an impersonal force at work within the work. Behind this myth of a poem being written "in everyone without anyone," the Surrealists revealed an entirely different experience, that of "the insecurity of the inaccessible..."[57] We will have to return to this luminous phrase ("the insecurity of the inaccessible"), less for the emphasis it places on the inaccessible — which always risks turning into brash heroism or into the heaven of the mystics —, than for this deep word of *insecurity*. Does all creation require insecurity?

From the writing foreign to me that pulsates in me, to the writing captured by many, the Surrealist exploration continued. *The Immaculate Conception*, a bizarre collection written in four hands by André Breton and Paul Éluard, was published in 1930. The titles of the first chapters, echoing the book title, boldly display their program: to confront the supernatural mysteries of (pro)creation together: "Man. Conception. Intra-uterine life. Birth." Proof also, if it were necessary, that the procreative fantasy dies hard, allowing here and there irreverent phonic games (ImmaCULée CONception) less blasphemous than gaily sexual.[58] Once again, automatic writing reveals the splendor of fulgurating and ephemeral poetic images, as beautiful as ... what can only live in the tear of a luster, between "being born" (to begin) and "being nothing."[59] "To be nothing. Of all the ways the sunflower loves light, regret is the most beautiful shadow on the sundial. Cross-bones, crosswords, volumes *&* volumes of ignorance *&* knowledge. *Where should one begin?*"[60]

Where in fact must we start so that these fortuitous encounters triggering writing, these coincidences of facts *&* of signs, unexpected events, "exquisite corpse" or even the "discovery," this "marvelous precipitate of desire," as Breton said, preside over the birth of a work?

The question is taken up with cheerful humor by the writer Julia Deck in her novel, *The Winter Triangle*. Its heroine, Mademoiselle, with the sweet, slightly dazed mien of one who struggles to understand the rules of productive life, tries to meet the requirements of her employment counselor in Le Havre, a city destroyed-rebuilt by some maniac of the ideal geometric square, in which she more or less lives. You have to

"be creative,"[61] asserts the counselor: motivation, rein-
tegration, versatility, mobility. Happy misunderstanding (objective chance?), creativity, Mademoiselle just
dreams of it, she who imagines herself as Bérénice
Beaurivage, photogenic novelist of a demanding and
somewhat confidential film by Eric Rohmer (a film on
the nuisances of architecture, let us note in passing).
Where to start, then? Through tea or the madeleine?
"She puts the cup down, opens her mouth, and stops
moving. No, dip the cake. Get her tea, get ready to
dip it in. Don't know anymore. Turns alternately to the
cup and the madeleine, giving them her most beautiful
jellyfish gaze." And here suddenly appears, as if out of
nowhere, a phrase whose rhetorical-poetic inventiveness (anaphora, alliteration, assonance, metaphor, ana-
coluthon & other paronomasia...) would have delighted a Chomskian linguist celebrating in the sixties "the
creativity of language":[62] "Crumbs rain down on his
jogging pants, between his feet where lie rubbish, buttons, bolts, bungs, blue Bic pen deprived of its cap."[63]
Who is the author of this sentence? Classic question.
The apprentice writer looking for her "notebook dec-
orated with rhinestone stars" to write it down? Or the
sentence that is written almost on its own through the
return (of the repressed?) of this automatic writing
which the Surrealists dreamed of? Is it the detritus that
collects alone, through phonic affinity (button, bolt,
bung), as in a childish refrain and falls back into the

sentence like drops *dripping* in Pollock's painting —
the painting, in a way, which is a drop by itself? A nod
or not to spermatic creativity, *dripping*, after piercing a
hole in the bottom of a bucket of paint, lets a stream
of color flow out (*pouring*) which then takes all the
undulations of the pendular movements imprinted
through the swing of the arm. Whoever hasn't seen
the painter Jackson Pollock (videos abound) standing,
leaning on his canvas stretched on the ground coming
to life in a rain of spurts *&* drips of paint that he pours
on it, doesn't know what creative climax is.

We must now understand the crisis of creativity in a
broader sense: the crisis of the creator subject or even
the crisis of the subject itself — grand post-traumatic
theme following World War I and which culminates
around the end of the sixties.[64] Thus Barthes, at the
height of the Structuralist period, evoked "the death of
the author": "It is language that speaks, not the author,"
he affirms. And he adds: "To write is, through a creative impersonality [...], to reach that point where only
language acts, 'performs,' *&* not 'me.'"[65] So make way
for the creative and anonymous power of language,
a bit like in the sentence of "buttons, bolts, bungs ...
cap," finally. Note the shift that Barthes operates: we
no longer speak of creative "personality" but of creative "impersonality." Once again, however, what does

"impersonal" mean? Drawing on the data of modern linguistics (especially the work of Benveniste) and extrapolating it to literature, Barthes echoed that language knows a "subject" (empty, apart from its enunciation), not a "person," in the humanist sense of the term.[66] *Exit* therefore the person and his subjective torments, his pretensions to creation. Make way for the "modern scriptor"[67] and his combinatorial activities, drawing from the infinite treasury of language the signs of a writing that nothing more allowed to qualify as "personal." Make way for multiple *writing*, an inexhaustible web of signs, with no origin other than Language (with a capital "L"). So we would therefore have finished with that theological-paternal notion of creation according to Barthes *&* his "Author-God"? Surrealism, he wrote in the same article, "in accepting the principle *&* the experience of a writing of the many, has contributed to desecrating the image of the Author." So be it. Barthes was well aware, however, that, under the guise of non-personal writing, one reactivated not exactly "the whispering immensity" of "wandering speech" as in Blanchot, but the infinite powers of Literature, another name for him of an irreducible sacred. The melancholy of the late Barthes, his inability to take the place of the author declared dead or to invent a lasting one, suggests that the crisis of the humanist subject was deep within him and perhaps without remedy.

Another dimension of the impersonal, more joyously iconoclastic subject: the conception through the Deleuze-Guattari duo of a new mode of creative writing for two, but ... without author: an unprecedented mode of generation, that of a "trans-subjective" work, as they said at the time, finally detached from any Œdipal phantasm and its heavy "familialism." Deleuze, a philosopher, disappointed lover of psychoanalysis, & Félix Guattari, a psychoanalyst turned philosopher,[68] both cultivating a certain minority path in their respective disciplines, both shocked witnesses of political and cultural revolutions of the second half of the 20th century, that of minorities and of dissidences, and who invented a strange subject sans ego: Deleuze-&-Guattari. In these major books written as a duo, *Anti-Œdipus* (Minuit, 1972) and *A Thousand Plateaus* (Minuit, 1980), they explore what they call hecceities: pre-individual, non-personal singularities. "A season, a winter, a summer, an hour, a date, have a perfect individuality lacking nothing, even though this individuality is different from that of a thing or a subject. They are *hecceities*, in the sense that they consist entirely of relations of movement and rest between molecules or particles [...]. A degree of heat, an intensity of white, are perfect individualities."[69] Who is then the subject of the writing? The question may no longer arise in these terms.

Speaking of his encounter with Guattari, the way in which they "understood and complemented, deper-

sonalized and singularized — in short, loved — one
another," Deleuze evokes the hostility that *Anti-Œdipus*
sometimes aroused upon its release. The fact that the
book was written as a pair is probably not unrelated,
according to him, because people like "assignations":
"So they try to disentangle inseparable elements and
identify who did what. But since each of us, like anyone else, is already various people, it gets rather crowd-
ed."[70] Life is not something personal, repeats Deleuze.
The impersonal here is neither anonymity nor the collective subject that would sign with one voice (we do
not replay the Surrealists' fascination with the Commu-
nist revolution). What they produce, what they create
strictly speaking, is precisely the invention of another
mode of subjectivization in writing. Deleuze's texts
(or Deleuze-Guattari, as one wishes, but in the books
that he writes alone Deleuze also succeeds in the tour
de force of being the singular name of a plurality of
subjects) on the new impersonal desiring subjectivi-
ties are so beautiful that we would like to quote them
all. Just this one then: "Saying something in your own
name is very curious; because it is not at all when one
thinks of oneself as a self, a person, or a subject, that
one speaks in one's name. On the contrary, an individual acquires a true proper name, at the end of the
most severe exercise of depersonalization, when individuals open themselves to the multiplicities that cross
right through them, to the intensities that run through

them."[71] Their dual books, and Deleuze's own books, arrange intersecting constellations of voices in sets of modular series; for example, the thirty-four series of *Logic of Sense* or the cartographic organization of *A Thousand Plateaus*.[72] Repetition and variation rather than the linear unfolding (historical and progressive) of an argument. Philosophy, precisely, has too often been recounted as the family romance of concepts, retracing the genealogy of their birth, their transmission by descent. We remember the pleasantly devastating charge of Deleuze against the history of philosophy, that "formidable school of intimidation," fabricating specialists in thought: "It played the role of repressor: how do you think without having read Plato, Descartes, Kant, and Heidegger, and the book of such and such on them? [...] An image of thought, called philosophy, has arisen historically, which perfectly prevents people from thinking."[73]

Yet, creation for Deleuze is by no means a personal and solitary invention (the philosopher in his ivory tower). His work with Guattari? A reciprocal betrayal, creating thoughts through slipping, shifting, breaking, even misinterpretation: "Each falsifies the other, which is to say that each of us understands in his own way notions proposed by the other. A well-thought-out series with two terms takes shape."[74] Each understands "in their own way": let us savor the apparent lightness of the expression, its casualness, like a challenge to

the traditionally fixed laws of philosophical discussion
which guarantee the truth of knowledge (Socratic dialogue), of its patrimonial construction, its academic
recognition, its transmission to future generations. To
create concepts is therefore to deviate from the rules,
to tamper with them as we say of a lock. The philosopher according to Deleuze is a deviant: he steals ideas,
borrows without warning, from behind, betrays. This
is how the history of philosophy is conceived, "as a
kind of sodomy or, what amounts to the same thing, an
immaculate conception [in which we find, curiously,
the Breton-Éluard duo...]. I imagine taking an author
from behind, and giving him a child that would be his
own and yet monstrous."[75] With this theory of creative
treason, it's the commonly received idea of the conception of a work that is undone. Who gave birth to
what, exactly? Whose artwork is it the child of? This
is not my body of writing ...

What remains then of the idea of a dual (male)
creative conception? If belief in a subject of creation
collapsed [*effondrée*] somewhat in the twentieth century (or *collapsed* [*effondée*], as Deleuze says, that is, it has
become deprived of a grounding),[76] it remains that the
men whose works I am referring to here, these writ-
er-philosophers (Deleuze, Blanchot, but also Foucault),
have in my opinion not only upset the limits between
the disciplines (literature, philosophy, psychoanalysis,
history...) but have created among themselves the un-

precedented space of a work: a virtual work no doubt, in that it is nowhere assembled or readable as such. An impersonal work at least in that it does not belong to any of them. If we wanted to give it a name, we could call this space, that of "inter-writing" ["*s'entre-écrire*"], in a sense no doubt close to what Blanchot called "discussion" [*entretien*], particularly in *The Infinite Conversation* [*L'Entretien infini*]. You never know who is speaking in Blanchot, or to which interlocutor (undefined, impersonal, and always as absent, even dead) he is speaking.[77] What is going on here? An original form of creative friendship, written at a distance, without individual partners, in a style that mixes the impersonal of philosophical or literary criticism and the subjective intimacy of private emotion. I trace the outlines of a space that I am bringing together here in its disparity, to indicate what could be the creative crisis of the subject at work in this inter-writing, the astonishing plasticity of its unstable movement.

If we try to circumscribe this space, we first find two articles by Michel Foucault, "The Thought from Outside" in 1966, about Maurice Blanchot, & "Theatrum Philosophicum" in 1970, about Gilles Deleuze.[78] Then two books which Deleuze and Blanchot, almost simultaneously, although at a distance from each other, devoted to Foucault after his death in 1984. Deleuze published a collection of studies soberly titled *Foucault* (Minuit, 1986) followed by some interviews on the phi-

losopher given to various newspapers the same year &
republished in *Negotiations*. Also in 1986, Fata Morgana
published a brief and dense short book by Blanchot entitled *Michel Foucault As I Imagine Him*. Texts scattered
therefore, apparently occasional texts (the publication
of books, the death of a man), but which only take on
their meaning and intensity when brought together for
a moment in their disparity. One does not write *to* the
other (this is neither a direct address, nor a personal
dialogue), nor does one write *about* him (in the form
of a critical review of his texts, despite appearances, or
work-to-work dialogue). To write to each other is also
to be understood in the sense that Deleuze said, in his
writing with Guattari, "we do not work together, we
work between the two."[79] I do not intend here to analyze these often celebrated texts, nor above all to make
a history of philosophy; rather, I want to show how
they fit together loosely, aggregating or unraveling in
provisional and flexible forms that allow us to envision
in another way a creation without a defined person.

Thus when Foucault writes his article "The
Thought from Outside" around Blanchot, for him it
is not a question of commenting on this or that text by
Blanchot (even if it evokes *Aminadab, The Most High,*
or *The One Who Was Standing Apart From Me*, for example). He does not address himself to Blanchot, he
writes through Blanchot's thought, which he pursues
& extends beyond him since, as he says: the "thought

from outside" is a "breakthrough to a language from which the subject is excluded." Blanchot, moreover, is not only one of the witnesses to this thought, says Foucault: "So far has he withdrawn into the manifestation of his work, so completely is he, not hidden by his texts, but absent from their existence and absent by virtue of the marvelous force of their existence, that for us he is that thought itself — its real, absolutely distant, shimmering, invisible presence, its inevitable law, its calm, infinite, measured strength."[80] It is easy to understand, reading Foucault, that this is by no means the hyperbolic recension of an admirer. It is not of the man Blanchot that he speaks (he does not know him) nor of the author Blanchot, so much has Foucault also deconstructed the humanist and personal notion of author. The author, he repeats, is a "transdiscursive" position; the great authors (Marx, Freud, in his example) are those "who cleared a space for the introduction of elements other than their own..."[81] Foucault sketches here the lines of this space.

From Foucault's text on Deleuze, we have in general especially retained the famous phrase: "One day, perhaps, the century will be Deleuzian."[82] Here I can only see one trait that strikes me: over the course of the text — it seems to me that this is one of the rare examples — Foucault's style loses its literary flamboyance, which is sometimes a bit haughty in adopting the Deleuzian verve and humor. In a frenzied finale where he makes stupidity and thought clash in a funny way, Foucault compares the effects of various drugs on thought. Thus the L.S.D.[83] that "reduces the dismal mimicry of stupidity to nothing" or the opium that lets the differences "arise & sparkle as so many minute, distanced, smiling, and eternal events." So, he concludes, wildly, "thought becomes a trance; and it becomes worthwhile to think." Deleuze has therefore reopened in his texts, emphasizes Foucault, the space of thought and it is again there, "springing forth, dancing before us, in our midst; genital thought, intensive thought, affirmative thought, acategorical thought."[84] Then comes to life on the stage of philosophical thought, once again vibrant and funny, the astonishing little theater of masks and puppets that a strange subject (let's call it "Foucault-Deleuze") summons to finish: "theater where, under the mask of Socrates, suddenly bursts the laughter of the sophist [...]. In the Luxembourg gatehouse, Duns Scotus pokes his head through the circular telescope; he wears a considerable mustache; it is that of Nietzsche, disguised as Klossowski."

After the death of Foucault, Deleuze like Blanchot evoked the silent creative crisis Foucault went through after the publication of the *History of Sexuality* in 1976. At that time, Foucault indeed interrupted the rest of the *History of Sexuality*, which was nevertheless planned. He stopped publishing books for eight years. Let us recall this in passing, without insisting: Deleuze recounts elsewhere that he himself wrote his first book quite early, "and then nothing for eight years. [...] It's like a hole in my life, an eight-year-old hole." And he adds, "That's what I find interesting in people's lives, the holes, the gaps, sometimes dramatic, but sometimes not dramatic at all. There are catalepsies, or a kind of sleepwalking over several years, in most lives."[85] Deleuze had known Foucault around 1962, when the latter was finishing writing *Birth of the Clinic*; he did not see him again in the last years of his life. Of this crisis in Foucault's life, Deleuze spoke with modesty and reserve; undoubtedly, he suggests, it was a crisis that was at the same time political, vital, and about thought. Besides, thought has never been a matter of theory but of life, he repeats. It is possible, however, that this time this crisis had been different from the others (Foucault had always been "seismic," proceeded by crises), "perhaps more depressive, more secretive, the feeling of being in an impasse?" These are only impressions, maybe it is quite wrong, he adds, but "I had the impression that he wanted to be left alone, to go where you could not follow him, save for some close friends."[86]

Blanchot too, in his book published after the death of Foucault, evokes the long silence that followed the publication of the first volume of the *History of Sexuality (The Will to Knowledge)*. He too willingly keeps at bay any overly simple or intrusive explanation of a man's life. He only suggests: "circumstances that I do not claim to elucidate because they seem to me to be of a private nature and besides it would be pointless to know them." Foucault, moreover, explained this in his preface to *The Use of Pleasure* (1984), "without quite convincing," he adds. Blanchot, however, hints at the hypothesis of a crisis, of an intimate upheaval that his illness must have provoked in him, but here again nothing can be simply stated; a certain insecurity of expression dominates Blanchot's formulation: "A personal experience I can only guess at and of which I believe Foucault was struck without then fully knowing what it meant (a strong body that stops being so, a serious illness that he barely anticipated, ultimately the approach of death which opens him not to anguish, but to a surprising & new serenity), his relationship to time and writing profoundly modified." [87]

Let us reread for a moment these "explications" given by Foucault in the introduction to *The Use of Pleasure*. He does not directly evoke any personal crisis, nor an *a fortiori* illness. Admittedly, this second book of the *History of Sexuality* appears "much later" than he had anticipated and "in a completely different form," but it advances a series of precisely argued justifications: long and patient historical research, a plunge into the archives of Greek and Latin Antiquity (languages and cultures of which he is in no way a specialist) and above all a "theoretical displacement" in relation to his initial project. Finally, he adds this, the elegant duplicity of which we will admire: "What would the value of the passion for knowledge be if it resulted only in a certain amount of knowledgeableness and not, in one way or another, and as much as possible, in the knower's self being bewildered? There are times in life when the question of knowing if one can think differently than one thinks, and perceive differently than one sees, is absolutely necessary if one is to go on looking and reflecting at all. I might be told that these games with oneself would better be left backstage [...]. The 'essay' — which should be understood as the assay or test by which, in the game of truth, one undergoes changes, and not as a simplistic appropriation of others for the purpose of communication — is the living body of philosophy [...]."[88] We will not comment on the gnarled complexity of a sentence that denies all confidence even as it delivers it. We will confine ourselves to remarking on three things: first that, faithful to his usual repugnance in the face of any idea of a confession, but also playing on those subtle retractions of writing that he admires in Beckett,[89] Foucault reaffirms the necessary oscillation between truth and lie (this is already what he said at the beginning of his article on Blanchot in 1966). Moreover, if knowledge must also "ensure ... the bewildering of the one who knows," we must understand "bewildering" in all senses of the term by the author of the *History of Madness*: the false road but also the risk of madness or collapse. Finally, it should be noted that, far from contradicting or judging in advance the hypotheses of Deleuze and Blanchot, it gives them a strange anticipated resonance, putting under the sign of bewilderment both the theoretical discourse and the body of the researcher himself, as we see.

But first, what happened to the relationship between Blanchot and Foucault? From the opening of his brief volume, *Michel Foucault As I Imagine Him*, Blanchot answers the question in simple but complex terms, as is his custom: "A few personal words. Precisely, I remained with Michel Foucault without knowing him intimately. I never met him, except once in the courtyard of the Sorbonne during the events of May 1968, perhaps in June or July (but I was later told that he was not there), when I addressed a few words to him, he himself unaware of who was speaking to him (whatever the detractors of May say, it was a splendid moment, when anyone could speak to anyone else, anonymously, impersonally, a man among men, welcomed without any other justification than that of being another person)."[90] One could not better indicate the impersonal of a dialogue forging the essential proximity and irreducible absence, as if playing in advance the final separation that would mark the death of Foucault through rendering it, as always with Blanchot, uncertain and as unstable. Hence the deliberately romantic recourse (in this writing at once distant *&* voluptuous that constitutes in my eyes the mark of Blanchot) to an imaginary portrait of Foucault, a portrait of the absent writer-philosopher, similar to the central void of the absence of the king in Velázquez's painting *Las Meninas*, which Foucault studied in the first chapter of *Words and Things*. Here again, without returning to the analyses of Foucault's work which Blanchot offers throughout his book, I only want to cite the end, overwhelming in my eyes in the revelation of that heartbreak at a distance that he always calls "friendship." "Friendship was perhaps promised to Foucault as a posthumous gift [...]. In bearing witness to a work demanding study (unprejudiced reading) rather than praise, I believe I am remaining faithful, albeit awkwardly, to the intellectual friendship that his death, so painful for me, today allows me to declare to him, as I recall the words attributed by Diogenes Laërtes to Aristotle: *O my friends, there is no friend.*"[91]

We can remember here the heartbreaking definition (or fastidiously bypassed, as we like) given by Blanchot of friendship, speaking after the death of Bataille, of that which continues to bind them together: "The pure interval which, from myself to this other, measures everything that there is between us..."[92]

Of his personal relationships with Foucault, Deleuze said either nothing or very little. He evokes that curious and apparently obsolete notion of a "fearsome kinship of souls..."[93] Taking up the difference that Foucault draws between love and passion in a 1981 interview, Deleuze in turn defines passion as "a sub-personal event which can last as long as a lifetime," "a field of intensities which indicates an individual without subject," unlike love, which is a relationship between people.[94] Passion, said Foucault in this interview with Werner Schroeter, is an always mobile state, "a kind of unstable moment that continues for obscure reasons, perhaps through inertia." In passion, "one is not oneself. Being oneself no longer makes sense."[95] We see how, from these generally banal remarks made by Foucault during an interview, Deleuze creates a quasi-concept that radicalizes its scope. Taking up this distinction elsewhere, he declares of Foucault: "I was in a certain state of passion for him."[96]

On a single point, Deleuze is categorical: it is stupid to believe in an alleged "return to the subject" in the later Foucault based on *The Use of Pleasure*. He repeats it over & over: "It's so stupid to hear it said: he realized he was wrong, he had to reintroduce the subject. He never reintroduced the subject." Besides, he emphasizes, Foucault never uses the word subject in the sense of a person or of a form of identity; he speaks of "new modes of subjectivation" as a process devoid of identity, of "Self," as the relationship of force with oneself. In short, for Deleuze, subjectivation in Foucault is part of the Blanchovian topology of "outside space," space to be conceived as "moving matter animated

by peristaltic movements, folds *&* foldings that consti-
tute [...] the inside *of* the outside." At this stage, all of
Foucault's thought becomes for him a "carnal or vital
topology."[97]

One can find luminous and true these lines of
Deleuze conjoining in the same final constellation the
"Outside" of Blanchot *&* the processes of Foucauldian
subjectivation under the sign of folding. We can also
(some did not deny it) find them questionable, even
betraying the thought of the final Foucault. It was forgetting the Deleuzian legitimacy of reading through
"sodomy" *&* its stories of a monstrous child. Above all,
it was not understanding that Deleuze was not mak-
ing an interpretive reading of Foucault; he wrote it
down, casting through anticipation Foucault and his
processes of subjectivation into the baroque space of
folds and foldings which he would deploy two years
later in his book on Leibniz (*The Fold: Leibniz and the
Baroque*, 1988). This "vital or carnal topology" that he
describes is also a Deleuzian space. In my opinion, this
should be seen as another definition of the creative crisis. Moving between Blanchot and Foucault, leading
them at full speed in his creation of nomadic spaces,
Deleuze with his usual virtuosity (which only appears
superficial to those who do not see the overwhelming depth of his erudite folds), annexes Foucault and
Blanchot in a mobile and fluctuating configuration, a
"passionate field of intensities" that would be named

"Deleuze-Foucault-Blanchot" — undoubtedly precisely that space which, in the introduction to *The Use of Pleasure*, Foucault called not the history of philosophy but "the living body of philosophy."

What is a fold, finally, according to Deleuze? A traversal of crises. Thus the Baroque, he recalls, is the exit from a long moment of crisis in which the collapse of the world of classical reason occurred. This collapsed because, like Descartes, it ignored the curvature of matter, its springs of vitality, its elasticity.[98] Yet, the characteristic of the Baroque is precisely to have conceived the overflowings of space and the tendency of matter to reconcile with fluid. Then bodies become flexible and pliant in continuously varying settings of matter.

I wrote above that it was necessary to resist the seduction of a too simple coupling between "crisis" and "creation," under penalty of seeing their positions exchanged in vain in an endless turnstile: crisis of creativity / creativity of crisis. I will now add that that risk of a sterile turnstile only exists if one fixes the oppositions in a rectilinear and oriented course, a simply resolving dialectic. "To detach oneself from oneself," as says Foucault, requires ceasing to think of oneself as a subject, endowed with a fixed identity, with a fixed intention to work. The crisis of creation arises precisely when the creative process becomes immobilized as a subject.

It is certainly not given to everyone to be able to endure the instability, the insecurity required by all creation, the forces of deformation (of bewilderment...) that it unleashes, indeed also the indisputable ecstasy that incites its reversals. The danger here again is to reduce its infinite folding processes to mechanical reversibility.

A real risk indeed borders the very movement of all creation, that of calcification, of the progressive petrification of the processes in play. One must probably be endowed with an extraordinarily plastic and malleable pulsional force to resist the solidifications in which the creative processes threaten always to atrophy. We are well aware of the tensions wherein those who think of themselves as creative subjects are at risk of remaining paralyzed: paranoiac diagrams believing to detect everywhere doubling and power struggles, power seizures and theft of ideas, or even sadomasochistic scenarios tirelessly repeated as identical. Deleuze used to say that only great writers (artists, philosophers) are capable of confronting forces too powerful for them in order to "liberate life."[99] Little writers (artists, philosophers) on the other hand, one might add, paralyze in narrow reversibility the power of the disfigurement of all creation. Do we want an example? The ecstasy of humiliation (to be understood in the reversibility of a double genitive)[100] in some current practitioners of auto-fiction (humiliate/be humiliated), or again, variant:

the ecstasy of persecution (same reversibility) in this or that writer who is alternately anti-Semitic and passionately Philosemite. Speaking of false claims of Jewish identity, Pierre Pachet once said to me mischievously: "To be Jewish, for some, is an infinitely desirable story..." In such blocked ecstasies, creative impulses sometimes founder.

CREATIVITY OF CRISIS

What should we finally understand in the much eroded term of "crisis" or rather, how to reactivate listening to it so much that its power of trepidation seems blunted, as if the crisis, in view of the endless rehashed list of the upheavals announced, has become our daily horizon? Global, ecological, crisis of landmarks, of family, of politics, crisis of meaning... We never stop reciting the litany of its various forms. Let us retain this definition for the moment: crisis is separation, rupture of equilibrium. Already, in Hippocratic medicine in ancient Greece, the crisis (*krisis*) designates the crucial phase in the evolution of a disease toward aggravation or recovery, the moment when the equilibrium teeters without one yet discerning in what sense: decisive moment of uncertainty. The term is related to *kritikos* (capable of discernment), derived from the verb *krinein* (to separate, to choose, to decide). In this sense, the crisis refers to criticism: discerning the disease, deciding on treatment. Yet could we imagine a crisis continuing indefinitely, without resolution or denouement? A crisis that would not close with a decision?

Apparently far removed from medical semiology, the three authors I want to mention here — Artaud, Beckett, Nietzsche — are no strangers to it. Not only because the three of them were confronted with the more or less severe risk of psychic collapse, but because their works have a singular link to the idea of crisis. In this sense, they can help us to better understand the so strangely indissociable relationship between crisis and creation — as if, contrary to popular belief, we only wrote at the cost of a preserved imbalance, in the endurance of insecurity. Should we then cultivate insecurity? Such a slogan would obviously appear shocking nowadays when the word "security" is so constantly called in to preserve our daily comfort, to allay our anxieties and fears, whether individual or collective. Who would dare to praise insecurity, however creative it is?

However, we should be careful not to associate crisis & catastrophe too quickly.[101] The imbalance can be barely perceptible without ceasing to be deep, far from the tumults and noisy outbursts that one imagines among the insane, far from the social or political earthquakes heralding cataclysms. The disruption of balance that marks the crisis is sometimes of low intensity; it speaks in a low voice, persists in a low decibel. So Joyce saying of *Ulysses* that a thin sheet of paper separated the book so skillfully and patiently constructed ... from madness. What are we talking about then, exactly? Of the invention of a precarious imbalance always on the verge of breaking but which beckons and which holds. Thus, the "Nerve Meter" of Artaud, the fold of Deleuze (or Leibniz-Deleuze), the Mallarméan "suspens," the Nietzschean aphorism ... Why "imbalance"? Because, if it is broken, two risks arise: on the one hand, that of regained balance, the return to the normal (even to normality), to ordinary life; on the other, the collapse, the fall, madness.

Thus, with Artaud, the "Nerve Meter" of the early texts draws the dreamed writing of a body whose disjointed elements are rejoined for a moment, held in the suspense of a breath. It's this movement of ephemeral but tenacious vibration that indicates the strange phrase that he invents: the "Nerve Meter." Not the stable connection that operates discursive thought but the tiny rhythms of a corporal language, its nervous ramifications, its suspended balance, always on the verge of rupture but not yielding to it. Artaud tirelessly pursues the incarnation in writing of the fragile suspense that is the "Nerve Meter." Thus, for example in his poem "Uccello, the Hair," he traces the features of a double, Paolo Uccello, the Florentine painter of the Quattrocento. He places it at the heart of the vibrating universe that brushes the bristles of his brush. For Artaud, Uccello is much more than a painter; he is a high wire artist, a tightrope walker on the intertwining wires where he draws himself patiently rewiring the tear between the world and himself. The bristles of the brush outline the fine lines of bristles, hair, and wrinkles uniting man & the world with the same thin wire: "the vibrating eyelash of things," "the infinite musicality of nerve waves."[102] This "Nerve Meter" silently animates the early texts of Artaud. This, for example: "To think without minimal rupture, without pitfalls in thought, without one of those sudden retractions to which my marrow is accustomed..."[103] Slight vibration of these words — "*sudden* retractions" — that must be captured on the fly in the hesitation of the double meaning called phonic ambivalence: retractions at once endured, experienced (a rupture suffered), and instantaneous, overwhelming (a sudden rupture).[104] We can see how, in order to grasp the two meanings of the word in the same rhythm, the slight tremor that animates them, we must not fear the creative insecurity that destabilizes Artaud's texts.

And likewise, ten years later, the Theater of Cruelty is a theater of crisis, continuing the exploration of the same rifts, inventing tense imbalances. During the conference "The Theater and the Plague" that Artaud gave at the Sorbonne in 1933 — a critical date if ever there was one in history — he declaimed with a hallucinated eloquence his theory of an organic theater reenacting the ravages of the plague. What is the plague? "... an illness that eviscerates the organism and life to the point of sparagmos and spasm..." In this sense, "theater like the plague is a crisis that is resolved by death or by healing."[105] Artaud, it should be noted in passing, is not very good at healing ... And how can the theater measure up to the disaster which threatens to affect all of society? He believes in the power of theatrical magick and its exorcisms. 1933: the rise of fascism throughout Europe; in Germany, Hitler is appointed chancellor. Among many others, the philosopher Edmund Husserl was excluded from all academic activity by virtue of anti-Semitic legislation. In 1935 in Vienna he gave a conference entitled "The Crisis of European Humanity & Philosophy" in which he analyzed the ethico-political crisis that traversed Europe like a profound crisis of reason. Everywhere, he emphasizes, "innumerable symptoms of the breakdown of life" ("this generalized collapse of life," said Artaud) are accumulating. Faced with this threat of "a fall into hostility toward the spirit and into barbarity," Husserl calls for "a heroism of reason" that would re-found a community of philosophers.[106] The heroism of reason just like the exorcisms of Artaud will prove to be appallingly helpless. The pendulum has fallen on the side of death.

The plague according to Artaud was obviously not foreign to that brown plague that was about to sweep across Europe. In a text published in 1946, shortly after the end of the war and his release from the asylum, he repeated that he, Artaud, had nevertheless loudly announced everywhere those wars and massacres, that unspeakable barbarism into which humanity had just

crossed: "For since 1918 who, and it wasn't in the theater, has hurled a probe 'into all the lower depths of
chance and of luck,' if not Hitler that unclean Mol-
dovan-Wallachian of the race of innate apes. Who
appeared on the stage with her belly of red tomatoes,
rubbed with garbage like parsley is with garlic, who with
bites of rotary sawmills has drilled into human anatomy.
Because room was left for him on all the stages of a still-
born theater. Whoever declares the Theater of Cruelty
utopian is going to have his vertebrae sawn off in the
stagings of barbed wire." I have spoken, he concluded,
"of real cruelties, ... of the molecular warfare of atoms,
frieze horses on all fronts, I mean drops of sweat on the
forehead, I was put in an insane asylum."[107] A moving
sentence from an "insane person" who still believes in
the omnipotence, in the magickal efficacy, of the sign.
Certainly. Are we sure that philosophical reason was
of greater help at the time?

This crisis that Artaud saw emerging from all sides
in the 1930s, threatening to contaminate the world, is
obviously also the one he lived in the depths of his being, that intimate disaster, that cut between the world
and himself, between himself and others. The crisis
is that separation. He repeats it in his very first texts:
"I can say, me, really, that I am not in the world"; or
even: "I assist myself, I assist Antonin Artaud." My life
has become a spectacle, I see myself playing it and the
experience is terrifying. Pure projection of a schizo-

phrenic (*schizein*: "to cut") who sees his discomfort invading the world? He invokes the superior lucidity of the "authentic madman" as he says, this new *Seer* who came after Rimbaud and all those hallucinated poets that he claims as his brothers: Lautréamont, Edgar Poe, Nerval, Hölderlin, Nietzsche ... So, he repeats it: we are cut off from reality, separated from the vital source of creation... Why? Because we live as if we are at the theater, as if life is a theater. This is another device that we must invent, a Theater of Cruelty where the cut between stage and hall, actor and spectator, world and its performance, will be effaced. He repeats it in his letters: I said cruelty as I would have said appetite for life, energy, vibrations, intensity. No longer the free and "digestive theater" of today but a theater reconnecting with vibrational matter in which each body is inscribed: a corporal and living theater. Let us add: a theater which is an act, that of the maintained imbalance. In a text published in 1935, "The Theater and Culture," which will serve as a preface to the *Theater and its Double*, he protests again against "the separate idea that we have of culture, as if there were culture on one side *&* life on the other; and as if real culture is not a refined way to understand and exercise life."[108] The inverse of separation? The burn. Life? "This kind of fragile and stirring hearth that forms do not touch." And the text concludes: "And if there is still something infernal and truly cursed in this time, it is to linger

74

artistically on forms, instead of being like victims burnt at the stake, signaling through the flames."[109]

For Artaud, the figure of the burned sacrificiant obviously refers to Carl Dreyer's film *La Passion de Jeanne d'Arc*, which was shot in 1927 &, in particular, the famous scene where the body of Joan, gradually consumed by the flames, slowly wilts on her pyre as he hands her a gigantic cross. This posture of the artist as a sacrificial figure is something Artaud will often return to at the end of his life: He, Artaud, is the Christ who gives his life to save men; the other is only an impostor. Above all, "signaling" is imperceptibly duplicated: not only to direct to the other an appeal but also to embody those signs vibrating in the burning of bodies, to become through the burn an animated body-sign.

We find in Samuel Beckett this same observation of separation, of recurring *schize*, life becoming an absurd spectacle of which I understand nothing. What do they want from me in the end and what is my place in this story? Who is this impotent Creator, this incompetent playwright who forgot to write my part? It's a leitmotif of many of Beckett's characters, and indeed in *Anti-Oedipus* Deleuze and Guattari call him, jokingly, with a certain complicit tenderness, "Beckett the schizo." Even if, naturally, Beckett does not share Artaud's delirium, one detects in him, transfigured by laughter, a near anguish, a feeling of radical strangeness that resurfaces regularly. Suddenly, the real becomes detached and I have the feeling of being separated from myself and the world, of being definitively at the spectacle. Thus, the duplication in which I watch myself act, where I hear myself speak, is one of the major themes of *The Unnamable*, a novel written in French in 1949, a year after the death of Artaud. There we find the question of the crisis (of the novel, of the character, of life), of the strange cut between a body and a voice, between a subject and his double. One of the questions asked is precisely this: Who is speaking? What is this voice in me that says "I," which may or may not be mine: the voice of another who creates me by speaking me? My own voice that I don't recognize? Beckett apparently laughs at it (yellow or bitter laughter, as he puts it) but his question really is this: Who speaks when I say "I"? Who is the subject of creation? Questions that Blanchot and Foucault will take up when they reread Beckett. Also, this one is not far, via his "characters" or his doubles, from saying, like Artaud: "I attend to myself, I attend to Samuel Beckett."

A famous passage in *The Unnamable* develops, between falsely naive incredulity and increasing disquiet, that feeling that life is no longer a dream but a spectacle which one attends slightly dazed: "oh you know, oh you, I suppose the audience, well well, so there is an audience, it's a public show, you buy your seat *&* you wait, perhaps it's free, a free show, [...] or perhaps it's compulsory, a compulsory show, you wait for the compulsory show to begin, it takes time, you hear a voice, perhaps it is a recitation, that is the show, someone improvising [...], before the curtain rises, that's the show waiting for the show [...]."[110] In Beckett, we often spend our lives waiting for something to happen, for someone to come on stage before realizing that it is too late, that nothing has happened, that no one has come, that the show is over, that life is over. Only the wait lasted, indefinitely stretched out. "[...] and the spectators, where are they, you didn't notice, in the anguish of waiting, never noticed you were waiting alone, that is the show for the fools in the palace waiting, waiting alone [...] for it to begin, [...] but where then is the hand, the helping hand, or merely charitable, or the hired hand, it's a long time coming, to take yours and draw you away [...]."[111]

Both a comical and a heartbreaking text that is like an illustration in action of Beckett's masterfully stumbling style, his art of imbalance. One of the hallmarks of Beckett's writing is in fact listening to French from a distance. Because no one better than an Irishman who will always cultivate that very slight quirk that he hears in French, can resonate with that double meaning of the word "assistance." English in fact has two words: *audience* (*assistance* in the sense of the public, spectators) and *assistance* (assistance in the sense of helping, providing relief).[112] It is on this equivocation that the text plays: attending a show, assisting someone (providing assistance). If there is assistance, why is no one reaching out to me and coming to help me? The text here plays on this quivering of meaning between separation (the cut between stage and auditorium) and connection (the helping hand). That famous "pious hand" in the old sense of "pious" which Beckett sometimes evokes is also that charitable hand which I expect but which I would violently refuse if it were to reach out to me. With Beckett, helping souls are often harpies who come to suck your blood with their supposed compassion. Variant of the imbalance held between hope and despair: the eternal question of Salvation and Redemption ceaselessly deferred (what is called Purgatory); or the expectation of the helping double that will come to my rescue (the Savior, the Father, Godot), which all kinds of messengers announce, but which never comes and which in any case I do not wait for.[113] Hence Beckett's recurring joke: I was born on the day the Savior died, too late for Salvation; all you have to do is "save yourself," or even "run away," in other words, *se sauver*.[114] Recurring games in *Waiting for Godot*: Save yourself! From what have you saved yourself again? Beckett's art of imbalance is expressed in this multiplicity of unstable forms, sometimes burlesque, sometimes more melancholic: oscillation, lullaby, back and forth, self-translation, moving fragments of words constantly in the process of being disassembled.

The Unnamable is the story (if we can call it a story) of someone, the unnamed "narrator-hero" ("unnamable" in every sense of the word), who hears a voice that he is not sure is his and which explores *in vivo*, one could say (but he is already almost dead), this crisis of the subject of creation. For example, this: "me I say what I'm told to say, that's all there is to it, and yet I wonder, I don't know, I don't feel a mouth on me, I don't feel the jostle of words in my mouth, and when you say a poem you like, if you happen to like poetry, in the underground, or in bed, for yourself, the words are there, somewhere, without the least sound, I don't feel that either, words falling, you don't know where, you don't know whence, drops of silence through the silence, I don't feel it, I don't feel a mouth on me..."[115] With Beckett, therefore, the source of automatic writing, the *dripping* of words that fall and drip on their own, seems to have dried up. The self-generation through paronomasia and phonic echo becomes lame, sluggish (poem, don't like; poetry, reads; word, subway ... "button, bolt, bung," finally, it was not so bad).[116] As he says funnily: "I don't feel the jostle of words in my mouth." What appears here is therefore quite another thing than surrealist flamboyance; it's an overwhelming and comical writing at the same time ("nothing is funnier than misfortune"), a writing of the fundamental insecurity of a stammering subject, tightrope walker staggering between being *&* not being *&* threatening always to miss his birth, and if he succeeds, to finally break his face. Standing up has become difficult, unless you end up crucified (Vladimir and Estragon in *Waiting for Godot* think for a moment they are the two thieves). The tightrope walker in Beckett keeps falling. We are a failing creation, he suggests. It began with the Fall and has been breaking down ever since. Creation is a divine slip that we are condemned to reproduce. A slip of the tongue (a lapsus), etymologically, is "the action of tripping" (from *labor*: slipping, falling). In the beginning was the Word, perhaps, but the tongue of God has split. A slip is a word that falls pitifully.

For Freud, as we know, far from being only a failure, the slip is a success of the unconscious. Something there has managed to cross the border of repression, to break through censorship and to say itself: an active process and not a simple failure. Failure is an indisputable form of creation, also for Beckett, who is perfectly familiar with the Freudian lesson: it is with this failing that we write.[117] It's that which he one day discovers, his "enlightenment" as he calls it, which is written with his idiocy, his stupidity, his inability to write. Writing well is within the reach of any good student (*Belles Lettres, l'Académie*). Writing badly is much more difficult. In other words, we don't write *contra* failing. We write, we create *with* failing. Here again, failing is not a state but a process, a dynamic. Beckettian failing is a creative energy, an imbalance in action. We must in fact distinguish two things: failure that is a result and failing that is an act, an implemented process. Repeated failure is a sign of neurosis. Freud calls the "repetition compulsion" the almost diabolical energy at the service of the death instinct that pushes us to tirelessly reproduce the same failures (always falling in love with the same type of partner who destroys us, falling back again and again in the same ruts). Psychoanalysts know what extraordinary energy certain subjects take to fail, to prevent themselves from moving forward, from succeeding, from living, from creating. However extraordinary its vigor, this energy is definitely on the side of stopping, of stagnation. The dynamic of failing, on the contrary, in the sense of the creativity of the crisis, is quite another thing. It is not at all a simple dialectical reversal. We do not see why failure would turn into success one fine day, we do not know by what simply reversed mechanism. Failing (this is what Artaud and Beckett discover, among others) is a creative process that forces us to rethink our overly simple categories of success and failure. Like failure, success is a standstill, it's a stasis, a result, if you will. That's why it's so disappointing sometimes to be successful. Success does not trigger anything and if some people collapse before success or after success (after a successful exam, for example), it's because success, like stasis, comes to an end. A goal has been reached ... and after? The dynamic is dead if we are not able to find, before this stasis of success (the achieved result), the dynamic that carried and that exceeded it.

Hence the final lines of *The Unnamable*: "I cannot go on, I will go on." In other words, I will continue to speak, to write... to keep this failing creation alive, this (desperate but funny) dynamic of failing. I will continue to exhaustion but exhaustion is infinite. Here too, with Beckett, exhaustion, as Deleuze has shown, is not fatigue.[118] Nothing to do with it. Exhaustion is infinite; it is a form of eternity. Eternity of damnation, as well, hence Beckett's tenderness for some of Dante's damned.

Let us note in passing that this theme of a crisis marked by the separation between the subject and his life frozen in spectacle, a frequent theme in Artaud or Beckett, will be found, displaced on the political field, in the writer and essayist Guy Debord, at the end of the '60s. In *The Society of the Spectacle*, a work in which some have detected a hyper-lucidity mixed with paranoia, Debord is inspired by the Marxist critique of the alienating separation between the worker and that which he produces; he broadens the analysis to the growing and almost schizoid unease experienced by those who live in an increasingly enslaving consumer society. "Separation" is analyzed there as a formidable power device. The first thesis of the book reads as follows:

"Everything that was directly lived has moved away into a representation."[119] Thus, commodity society only produces a subject-consumer estranged from his real desires. The 29 theses state for example what Artaud would not have denied in his most acute period of revolt against society: "The origin of the spectacle lies in the world's loss of unity, and its massive expansion in the modern period demonstrates how total this loss has been [...]. The spectacle divides the world into two parts, one of which is held up as a *self-representation* to the world, and is superior to the world. The spectacle is simply the common language that bridges this division. [...] The spectacle thus unites what is separate, but it unites it only *in its separateness.*"[120] With Debord and the Situationists, the analysis of the crisis of the subject in modern capitalist societies thus joins in many ways the diagnosis made by the writers that I speak of here: alienation, spectacle, separation, loss of the vital sense of life. The question is the same: how to become alive again?

Of course, the time in which Nietzsche lived, the end of the 19th century, is quite different; it is therefore not a question of evoking a historical approach to his relationship to the creative crisis. What matters to me here are two things: first of all to recall the immense influence of Nietzsche's philosophy on what has come to be called French thought of the second part of the 20th century, that of Foucault, Deleuze, Barthes, Blanchot, or Bataille, for example.[121] Then, to analyze the power of imbalance at work in the poetic & aphoristic style of Nietzsche. For Georges Bataille, who as always gives a slightly grandiloquent image of him, Nietzsche is a tragic hero of thought. In June 1939, he published a text, "The Madness of Nietzsche," which opens with a unique prose poem in the form of a tribute:

On 3 January 1889,
fifty years ago today,
Nietzsche succumbed to madness:
on Piazza Carlo-Alberto in Turin,
throwing himself sobbing around the neck of a horse
that had been beaten,
then he collapsed;
when he came to again he believed he was
DIONYSOS
or
CHRIST CRUCIFIED.
This event
should be commemorated
as a tragedy.[122]

Nietzsche, as Bataille essentially writes, went mad on our behalf; he gave us the gift of his madness, that "life-destroying exuberance," for to avoid collapsing in our turn.

This paradoxical alliance of vitality and destruction often took in the life of the philosopher the form of a long journey through multiple crises until his final collapse in Turin in 1889 and his silent death eleven years later in Weimar. Yet, nowhere better than in the writing of *The Gay Science* does this fundamental link of Nietzsche's writing of imbalance appear to me. It is generally accepted that *The Gay Science* inaugurates the last period of the work of the philosopher. The year 1882 was marked by the publication of the first four books of *The Gay Science* and he saw it as a sign of an end of the crises that had hitherto had a lasting effect on him. The previous year had indeed seen the resurgence of the disease that prevented him from writing and thinking: headaches and eye pains, which often kept him bedridden. In the foreword to the second edition of *The Gay Science*, he now describes himself as beset "by the *intoxication* of recovery." After the period of "severe illness" he had just underwent, he says he has returned regenerated "from such abysses," "returns *newborn*."[123]

In a remarkable way, *The Gay Science* exemplifies this singular Nietzschean writing that combines aphorism and poetic style. Even if the aphorism is not new to him (we already find it in *Human, All Too Human* in 1878 and in *Daybreak* in 1881), here he literally puts into action the breakdown, the crisis of thought. Deleuze, in the short book on Nietzsche that he published in 1965, chooses to open the presentation of the philosopher with these few lines that highlight the Nietzschean aphorism: "Nietzsche integrates two means of expression into philosophy, the aphorism and the poem. These very forms imply a new conception of philosophy, a new image of the thinker and of thought. For the ideal of knowledge, for the discovery of truth, Nietzsche substitutes *interpretation* and *evaluation*."[124] The aphorism is in effect constantly put at the service of logical breaks in reasoning, of pitfalls into which the reader is invited to fall if he expects to peacefully follow the logical thread of an argument. The aphorism is a power of error and of wandering, a force of failing that destabilizes the form of truth and meaning. The aphorism, if you will, is Nietzsche's "Nerve Meter."

Any reader of Nietzsche knows this painful sensation of losing oneself constantly in a contradictory, elusive discourse, the guiding thread of which is missing. A bit like when one tries to understand the logic of Artaud's speech, one often has the vexing impression of reading one thing & its opposite at the same time. In his fundamental work, *The Problem of Truth in Nietzsche's Philosophy*, Jean Granier also underlines what he calls the "vehement" proliferation of the contradictions that give the Nietzschean work "the appearance of a field of ruins." And he quotes this remark by Karl Jaspers, which is echoed by many commentators on Nietzsche: "All of Nietzsche's statements seem to be denied by others that also come from him. Self-contradiction is the fundamental trait of Nietzsche's thought."[125] Nietzsche for his part evokes the "experimental" character of his philosophy, a method by which he successively "tries" several hypotheses, by modifying the lighting, by varying the perspectives, until finding a kind of precarious balance that will shortly thereafter be subjected to another earthquake. In all cases it is a question of contesting a fundamentally dualistic metaphysical tradition that too calmly opposes good and evil, true and false, which reasons by antinomies, rigid contradictions, and considers the uncanny ambiguity of existence as an intolerable scandal. Paradoxically then, Nietzsche pleads for subtle transitions, a sense of nuance. It's thus how we can understand what he writes in *The Wanderer and His Shadow*: "*Habit of seeing opposites.* — The general imprecise way of observing sees everywhere in nature opposites (e.g. 'warm' and 'cold'), where there are, no opposites, but differences of degree. This bad habit has led us into wanting to comprehend and analyze the inner world, too, the spiritual-moral world, in terms of such opposites. An unspeakable amount of painfulness, arrogance, harshness, estrangement, frigidity has entered into human feelings because we think we see opposites instead of transitions."[126]

As Granier has abundantly shown, the conception of truth that Nietzsche fights is that of the reassurance against anguish. This is evidenced for example by the ironic parallel proposed in *The Gay Science* between the priest and the philosopher. I willfully neglect its successive reversals to temporarily stabilize the cruel portrait he offers of ecclesiastical wisdom. For the people, says Nietzsche, the priest is on the side of wisdom, of contemplative serenity, where the philosopher seems to be in the grip of the torments of uncertainty. But what is the wisdom incarnated in the priest? "This clever, bovine piety, peace of mind, and meekness of country pastors that lies in the meadow and *observes* life seriously while ruminating—"[127] Once again therefore, as with Artaud, the cautious spectator opposed to the actor burning at his stake, here in the guise of the philosopher in the throes of thought, living "in the stormy clouds of the highest problems." The wisdom of the priest would therefore be prudent renunciation of the danger of instability; to him and to his peers go the praises of the people, to those "sure" men who deliver us from uncertainty, to those contemplators who stand away from the frightening turbulences of life and provide simple answers to our requests for meaning. Yet precisely, what is "true" for Nietzsche covers above all the aspiration to permanence, ontological security; it's the wish for a world of reassuring stability, that of "eternal truths" which deliver us from our anxieties in the face of imbalances and disruptions in life. What do we ultimately ask the priest according to Nietzsche? To deliver us from the insecurity of life, to give us the grace of reasonable appeasement, to forbid us to think too much! The reverse, we see, of the teaching of Zarathustra, but he is neither a priest nor a sage. Zarathustra calls for betrayal, he never stops failing and being the laughing stock of men, he declines and he falls. The very opposite of all doctrine: praise of dancing and of insecurity. "I say to you: one must still have chaos in oneself in order to give birth to a dancing star."[128] In other words: deliver us from the certainties brandished by the priests and masters and we will have a chance, perhaps, of becoming creators.

We remember the figure of the tightrope walker, the rope-dancer, in the prologue to *Zarathustra*: he is the one who faces the risk of imbalance and who falls pitifully into the void in "a whirlwind of arms and legs." He falls, "torn and broken, but still alive," right next to Zarathustra. Then, the latter comforts the dying ("there is no Devil and no Hell"; "You have made danger your calling") and the tightrope walker weakly shakes his hand, "as if he were feeling for Zarathustra's hand to thank him." Man, Zarathustra teaches, "is a rope stretched ... over the abyss" (*Zarathustra*, Prologue, §4). Nietzsche's style (aphorism, discontinuity, fragmentation, paradoxes) is like this rope stretched over the void. The reader-tightrope walker attempts an uncertain crossing and is constantly on the verge of rupture. What, in this sense, is an aphorism? Etymologically, it is a definition, a delimitation (*aphorizein*, define). Originally, the aphorism was a sentence-like

phrase intended to define a concept, to sum up a received truth. We readily cite the example of this aphorism by Boileau: "Nothing is beautiful but the true: the
true alone is lovable" (*Epistles*, IX). Subsequently, the
term suggests on the contrary situating received truths
in a new light, to surprise, to confuse common sense.
The aphorism in Nietzsche breaks the habits of thinking, breaks the ordinary course of logic and of syntax.
For example, how to fight against stupidity? Not by developing well-argued criticism but rather by depriving
it of "its good conscience," by undermining its foun-
dations; Deleuze would say: by *collapsing* it. Nietzsche
calls this "doing harm to stupidity" (*The Gay Science*,
Book Four, §328). Because it is not only a question of
rising up against a metaphysics that would possess the
monopoly of discursive language, but of *collapsing* it,
of "deconstructing" it from the inside (if one will for-
give me this philosophical anachronism knowingly in-
voked). Truth is no longer to be sought but to be pro-
duced as a provisional interpretation: conflict, enigma,
tension, instability — separation without synthesis as
in Heraclitus.[129] No longer solidified, sacred, doctrinal
truth but the ephemeral and endlessly unfinished process of the creation of an interpretation. Crisis of truth,
no doubt.

It is easy to understand the risks of misunderstanding, or even misinterpretation, taken by such a
collapsing thought, cultivating within itself the crisis

of meaning and of truth. The misinterpretations and manipulations of Nietzsche's thought were immense, as we know. Few works, no doubt, were so betrayed, frozen in inept precepts (the will to power, the superman…), let alone the posthumous falsifications of his archives, or the use of his work for propaganda purposes by the Nazis. Even without it being a question of a will to harm or to betray, it suffices to read sometimes a few critical interpretations of the work to understand how difficult it is to comment on Nietzsche without stabilizing his thinking with impunity. A sole example, Peter Pütz's commentary on §26 of *The Gay Science* wherein Nietzsche lists some possible definitions of what living might mean.

> *What is life?* — Life — that is: continually shedding something that wants to die; Life — that is: being cruel and inexorable against anything that is growing weak & old in us, and not just in us. Life — therefore means: to be free of pity for the dying, the wretched, the old? Always being a murderer? — And yet old Moses said: "Thou shalt not kill!"

Pütz comments: "Nietzsche even opposes the 5th commandment of the Decalogue insofar as he does not conceive that one can live without always killing. An extremely disturbing maxim, and devastating in its ap-

plication [...]. It demands the most implacable harshness toward what freezes & wants to perpetuate itself
eternally. Living while killing means first & foremost:
surpassing oneself" (cf. §26).[130] We can better understand here the difficulty that we encounter when
we try to translate into simply affirmative terms what
Nietzsche "wanted to say." Nowhere in effect does he
give us a definition of what it means to live. He disso-
ciates a word from its context, isolates it between dash-
es, as if to better mimic the unequivocal definitions
that a given dictionary might proffer; he pushes these
definitions to the absurdity that they imply, contenting
himself with juxtaposing them without passing the least
judgment. No answer to the question, no simple definition, no logical reasoning. The question, between in-
terrogation, exclamation, and immense contradiction,
remains in imbalance, open to any interpretation. Living
is undecidable.

As a philologist, Nietzsche knows the extraordinary complexity of language, its slippages, its treach-
eries; he does not seek to reduce them, he plays with
them. Mallarmé, at the same time, did not say anything
else when he spoke of undoing syntax & inventing "a
new prosody," an unstable poetic language that opens
in words a "center of vibratory suspense." Thus in
"As for the Book" in 1895, evoking the incriminations
of certain readers, surprised by the absence of some
"planned swing of inversions," Mallarmé writes: "I prefer,

in the face of this aggression, to retort that some contemporaries do not know how to read — except newspapers; of course, those provide the advantage of not interrupting the chorus of preoccupations. To read — that practice."[131] The cut, the breaking of verse in Mallarmé's work, leaves the meaning suspended ("to suspend until the temptation to explain oneself"). It is obviously not a question of assimilating the writing of Nietzsche to that of Mallarmé but of being attentive in both of them to the creation of a volatile poetic writing, open to interpretation: fragmentary arrangement, aphorisms, blank areas, abrupt parallels, unresolved contradictions. The difficulty with suspension, like that of the rope-dancer (and we know of Mallarmé's love for dancing), is to hold out as long as possible without falling back.

"If it pleases one," writes Mallarmé again, "who is surprised by the magnitude, to incriminate … it will be Language, which here is the frolic." The *frolic* of language, as we say, the amorous frolics, the capers and frisky movements… that Mallarmé maliciously opposes, a few lines below, to the *debate*: "The debate — which the necessary average clarity deviates into a detail, the remains of grammarians."[132] The poetic frolic in the face of the debate of grammarians, logicians, metaphysicians… Here again, Nietzsche would agree; we know his resolute mistrust of grammar. Let us recall in passing the famous phrase from *Twilight of the Idols* §5: "I fear that we can never get rid of God, because we still believe in grammar."[133]

Nietzsche's dream: to be, not exactly a fold as in Deleuze, but a wave (although Deleuze would say that a wave is a fold, he who was delighted with the echo his book had won among surfers). Let us reread §310 of *Gay Science*, entitled "Will and wave." As often, Nietzsche plays on the paronomasia of two words in German; here *der Wille* (the will) and *die Welle* (the wave). "This wave," he wrote, "how greedily it approaches, as if it were trying to reach something! [...] It seems to be trying to arrive before someone else..." The very beginning of this fragment rests on the assimilation of *Welle* and *Wille*, the attribution of a will to the wave, apparently endowed with the intentionality of a human subject and which would give itself a mysterious purpose. The waves, personified (young girls or young women), are animated by desire (curiosity, envy), experience emotions (greed, disappointment, anger). Conversely, the will is like a wave, coming & going in the play of the surf, somewhat insecure or strengthening. Reciprocal contamination of *Wille* and *Welle*. "That is how the waves live — that is how we live, we who will! — I will say no more." There follows a strange *marivaudage* between the philosopher-poet contemplating the sea (posture of German romanticism if ever there was one...) and the reactions given to the waves: "So? You distrust me? You are angry with me, you beautiful monsters?" The temptation of seduction: tell me your secret! What do you want in the end? Let us translate: what is the will (the desire) of the wave-woman? "What does a wave want?" as Lacan would say. Thunderstorm and storm then stir the waves in anger (still romanticism...) until the final reversal: "How could I betray *you*? For — mark my words! — I know you, *&* your secret; I know your kind! After all, you and I are of the same species! — After all, you *&* I have the same secret!"

A sudden reversal of perspectives ("you and I, we are of the same species") that may surprise a reader insufficiently mobile or in too much of a hurry, incapable of bending to the destabilizing force of the aphorism, accustomed to seeking the meaning of a text as one would seek a solution with a riddle. What is required here, on the contrary, is that we embrace the movement of the text, its folds, its becoming-wave. May we be overwhelmed by it enough to grasp this: no longer are the waves like me, endowed with will and intention, but I am a wave subjected to the movement of the surf. So *der Wille* is no longer a psychological or moral will, but an apparently absurd, insane force (for what purpose is all this?), a power that animates and exceeds all human will: a "will to power" (*Wille zur Macht*: will *toward* power). In other words again: an irrepressible force of life, a desire, a pulsional drive as Freud says (cruelty, as Artaud would say). What Nietzsche calls in *Zarathustra*: "the vital, inexhaustible, and creative will."[134] What is unhinged in the animation of this aphorism is at the same time the belief in a sensible action, the work of a subject who is master of himself and who knows what he wants, but also faith in the power of unveiling a truth, the relief that it brings. In the end, we will know the secret, the meaning that it all had. And why not the meaning of life, while you are at it! You confuse the philosopher and the priest! Nothing is therefore given to us in the end: no solution to the enigma to appease us, none other than the one of which we can be the actor *&* the creator.

A bit like in Beckett: what meaning did it all have in the end, this waiting in vain, this dozing back and forth of a lullaby, this obstinate wandering, those impossible loves, this Purgatory that stretches toward infinity? Let us be careful not to immediately reclose everything in this overly simple word "absurd." Continue the quest, continue to miss the meaning, to miss (fail) better, Beckett repeats. This is not a test; there is no winner or loser, no salvation or damnation. And if we fall, it's often funny: finally an event! We fall like dice and words fall: failing is a creative experiment.

And in the same way, what Nietzsche suggests would be to learn to play, without any assurance, with the destabilizing force of interpretation-creation, its unstable movement, which gropes its way through the failing of meaning (no one knows exactly where he is going). It would be necessary here to be able to quote the whole paragraph of *Gay Science* entitled "Believers and their need for belief."[135] Faith, says Nietzsche, serves as a support, a crutch. However, the number of "solid" principles one needs in order to stand up measures a person's degree of weakness. This desire that we have for support, "this impetuous desire for certainty," is what keeps religions, metaphysics, dictatorships, powerful. "Which means," adds Nietzsche, "that the less someone knows how to command, the more he longs for someone who commands, who commands with severity, a god, a prince, a state, a physician, a father confessor, a dogma, a party conscience. [...] As soon as a man comes to the fundamental conviction that he *must* be commanded, he becomes a 'believer.'" What should we imagine on the contrary? A joy, a *freedom* to want. And here is the end of the paragraph: then "the spirit takes leave of all faith *&* every wish for certainty, practiced as it is in maintaining itself on light ropes and possibilities and dancing even beside abysses." Learn to dance, always. Learn to traverse the disequilibrium.

Interpretation was for a long time the exclusive domain of theologians, transforming texts into dogmas and precepts to obey: here is what must be understood, the rules to be followed rely on our reading, do not dare to invent another. We priests are the guardians of meaning. Let us imagine rather an interpretation that would constantly experiment, would walk through possible meanings, without the certainty of finding the last word on meaning. It would be, in the Nietzschean sense, to cultivate the art of interpretation as a power of instability, invention, creativity. In praise of creative imbalance, rejection of dictated dogmas and beliefs. A plea for the poetic and creative insecurity of those who, as Deleuze says, dare to plunge into chaos. "Art, science, and philosophy [...] cast planes over chaos. These three disciplines are not like religions that invoke the dynasties of gods, or the epiphany of a single god, in order to paint on the umbrella a firmament [...]. The philosopher, the scientist, the artist seem to have returned from the land of the dead."[136] In other words, not everyone is capable of facing this crisis that is creation.

Are we then definitively excluded from the cenacle, once again kept outside, simple spectators-consumers of creation, we "ordinary neurotics," as playwright Valère Novarina jokingly says, we readers, performers, passionate lovers of art and creation? We could evoke again what the Franco-American artist Louise Bourgeois has repeated all her life: "Art is a guarantee of Sanity." Let us add: for the artist as well as for those who replay their work with them. What Bourgeois constantly reckons in her works is very exactly the relationship that is difficult to find between balance and imbalance: scales in precarious equipoise, crutches straightening the flesh, weights and counterweights (softness and hardness, concave and convex, gigantic and minuscule, man and woman, architecture and body...), totem characters stuck in the ground, spiders erect on their slender legs, characters in horizontal levitation, clothes suspended from hangers, from trees, from vertical skeletons. "My sculptures," she says in an interview, "are infallible equations. The equations must be tested. Does the blood pressure drop, does the compulsion go away, does the pain give way? Either it works or it doesn't."[137] This is how she uses the fragments and debris of psychoanalytic myths (Oedipus, totemic repast, hysterical spasms, secrets and prohibitions hidden in the parents' room...) which she puts back on stage in her installations, not to illustrate them as themes and contents, but to use them as objects, plastic elements to modulate, to replay, and which she gives us to replay. Psychoanalysis is indeed present everywhere in her work since it is familiar to her. She carried out a long personal psychoanalysis, read a great deal of Freud and his successors, but we hardly advance (or even go around in circles) if we propose a psychoanalytic interpretation of the contents of her work. For her, psychoanalysis is a material like any other, an element of her life, just like her memories, her perfume bottles and spools of thread, her old clothes or old chairs, which she reuses in her creations.

What Bourgeois ultimately reminds us of is this: psychoanalysis is not a repertoire of themes and contents; it is to be experimented with. It is an emotional and vital experience. And so is modern art. The question in the past, when faced with a work, was: "What does it represent?" Then later: "What does it mean?" Art means nothing, Beckett also said in his inimitable way: "There is no painting [*peinture*]. There are only paintings [*tableaux*]. These, not being sausages, are neither good nor bad. All that can be said of them is that they translate, with more or less loss, absurd and mysterious pressures toward the image, that they are more or less adequate vis-à-vis obscure internal tensions."[138] Pushes and counter-pushes, imbalance in action. And the spectator? An actor of his vision, of his interpretation, of his wandering: how to face Bourgeois' "Cells" which half conceal their content, how to turn around, what angle of vision to construct? Bourgeois, like most contemporary artists and writers, forces us to experience the imbalances they have created, this unstable and often poignant oscillation between anguish and joy: a creative crisis to be crossed again, by each of us, if one has the strength. Again, not everyone is able to cope with this crisis of creative interpretation. A question of hypersensitivity, that is to say of emotional forces to engage and play with. Nietzsche calls this *evaluation* (not the search for the contents of truth): weight *&* measure, calculation of relations, precarious balance once again. As Zarathustra said: there is no value in itself, all value is created, experimented with, in the unstable balance of desire and rejection. "Evaluating is creating: hear this, you creators! Evaluating is itself the treasure & jewel of all valued things." [139]

ENDNOTES

1 Antonin Artaud, "Correspondence with Jacques Rivière" [1924], *Selected Writings* (California: Farrar, Straus and Giroux, 1976) 31–52; 35.

2 Alain Ehrenberg, *The Weariness of the Self: Diagnosing the History of Depression in the Contemporary Age* (Montreal & Kingston: McGill-Queens University Press, 2010) 130.

3 Edgar Morin and Thierry C. Pauchant, "For a Crisology," *Industrial & Environmental Quarterly*, Vol. 7, Nº 1 (1993) 5–21. The quote here attributed to McLuhan is actually by R.D. Laing: "Madness need not be all breakdown. It may also be break-through. It is potentially liberation and renewal as well as enslavement and existential death." See R.D. Laing, *The Politics of Experience and The Bird of Paradise* (Penguin, 1967; 1970) 110. For a further exploration of this notion of madness as break-through, see Deleuze & Guattari, *Anti-Œdipus* (MN: University of Minnesota Press, 1983) 130–137.

4 The economic processes described by Schumpeter combine destructive and creative effects in so far as they are linked, according to him, to the innovative dynamics of modern capitalism. Cf. Joseph Schumpeter, *Capitalism, Socialism, and Democracy* (New York; London: Harper & Brothers, 1942).

5 On the astronomical & metaphysical question of the "limits" of the infinite, see Alexandre Koyré, *From the Closed World to the Infinite Universe* (1957), in particular Ch. 11, 25–57.

6 See in particular Margaret Mahler, whose first work on the subject dates to the 1950s: *On Human Symbiosis and the Vicissitudes of Individuation: Infantile Psychosis* (New York: International Universities Press, 1968).

7 Melanie Klein, *Contributions to Psycho-Analysis* (1921–1945) (London: Hogarth Press, 1965), in particular, the chapter "Mourning and its Relation to Manic Depressive States."

8 Antonin Artaud, preface to *The Theatre & Its Double* [1935] (London: Alma Classics, 2010) 7.

9 D.W. Winnicott, *Playing & Reality* (1971; New York: Tavistock, 1982) 115–127. See also Frédérick Aubourg, "Winnicott et la créativité," *Le Coq-héron*, Vol. 173, Nº 2 (2003) 21–30.

10 Pierre Fédida, *Des bienfaits de la dépression. Éloge de la psycho-thérapie* (Paris: Éditions Odile Jacob, 2001) 10–16.

11 Roland Barthes, *The Preparation of the Novel. Lecture Courses and Seminars at the Collège de France* (1978–1979 and 1979–1980) (New York: CUP, 2011) 243.

12 André Gide, *Marshlands*, tr. Damion Searls [1895] (New York: NYRB, 2021).

13 Roland Barthes, *The Preparation of the Novel*, op. cit., 253. On a similar theme, the myth of the accursed writer and the mystique of suffering inherited from Christianity, see Pascal Brissette, *La Malédiction littéraire. Du poète crotté au génie malheureux* (Montréal: Presses de l'Université de Montréal, coll. « Socius, » 2005).

14 In France, it was the neuropsychiatrist Boris Cyrulnik who made famous the notion of resilience, in the sense of resistance, of a psychological rebound allowing certain individuals to be reborn after a trauma.

15 *Appareil*, Nº 13 (2014): https://journals.openedition.org/appareil/. See in particular the articles by Daniel Payot, « Les vacances du poète », and Jean-Louis Déotte, « Entre le trauma et le coma. Entretien avec Germain Roesz. »

16 Germain Roesz, *Peintures, 1970–2011* (Paris: L'Harmattan / Cour carrée, 2012); cited by J.-L. Déotte, *Appareil*, Nº 13, op. cit.

17 Pierre Guyotat, *Coma*, tr. Noura Wedell (California: Semio-text(e), 2010) 17.

18 Gilles Deleuze, *Logic of Sense* (New York: CUP, 1990) 148.

19 *Ibid.* In *Dialogues II*, where the quotation is repeated (1987) 65, it is linked without further details to two books by Bousquet, *Traduit du silence* and *Les Capitales*. In *Logic of Sense*, Deleuze refers to an article by René Nelli, a close friend of Bousquet, in *Cahiers du Sud*, N° 3 (1950). I admit that I do not find Bousquet's sentence anywhere in my books and everyone who quotes it is content to refer to Deleuze. This does not mean that it is apocryphal: it undeniably corresponds to some of the poet's aspirations. Above all, thus repeated everywhere thanks to Deleuze, it has the merit of granting Bousquet the stature he often doubted he would attain during his lifetime. As he wrote to Germaine, one of the women he loved: "[...] life is to be created. We find it prefigured on the road to dreams as a more beautiful form to be substituted, at the cost of all suffering, for the cold face of events" in *Lettres à Poisson d'Or* (Paris: Gallimard, 1967, reprint coll. «L'imaginaire,» 1988) 31. Later addition: Thanks to Jean-Baptiste Para and Alain Freixe, this is undoubtedly the key to the enigma. In his article, René Nelli writes: "My injury, he said, existed before me: I was born to embody it." This "he said" is omitted in Deleuze. The point would therefore be reported, even extrapolated from the work. Nelli does not provide the reference.

20 Gilles Deleuze, *Logic of Sense*, op. cit., 149.

21 Joë Bousquet, *Traduit du silence* [1941] (Paris: Gallimard, coll. «L'imaginaire,» 1995) 90.

22 Joë Bousquet, *Lettres à Poisson d'Or*, op. cit., 30.

23 Joë Bousquet, *Traduit du silence*, op. cit., 89.

24 *Ibid.*, 110. He adds: "My inner strength was my infirmity, in my absence from any real place."

25 Joë Bousquet, *Le Cahier noir* (Albin Michel, 1989; rééd. La musardine, 2018) 104, 106, and 171.

26   Joë Bousquet, *Traduit du silence*, op. cit., 258–259.

27   "You first saw the light of day the day Christ died and now." Samuel Beckett, *Company* (London: Calder, 1989) 12.

28   [TN] H.L.M. (Habitation à Loyer Modéré), created starting in 1950 in response to the postwar housing crisis, is low-income public housing. This French version of slums or ghettos constitutes 16% of all housing in France.

29   Louis Calaferte, *Septentrion* (Paris: Denoël, 1984; rééd. Gallimard, coll. Folio, 1990) 415.

30   *Ibid.*, 417.

31   A Sartrean-inspired exegesis could after all have interpreted Calaferte's guilt in terms of his being a traitor to his social class.

32   Jean-René Huguenin, *Journal* [1964] (Paris: Le Seuil, coll. Points, 1997), with an introduction by Renaud Matignon and a preface by François Mauriac, 294–295.

33   *Ibid.*, 230–231.

34   Maybe I'm going too far. Foucault limits himself to writing, which is already not so bad: "I imagine that there's an old memory of the scalpel in my pen. Maybe, after all, I trace on the whiteness of the paper the same aggressive signs that my father traced on the bodies of others when he was operating? I've transformed the scalpel into a pen." Michel Foucault, *Speech Begins After Death. In Conversation with Claude Bonnefoy* (2013) 39. We will note with curiosity this expression of "aggressive signs," far from any medical compassion.

35   Jean-René Huguenin, *Journal*, op. cit., 302.

36   *Ibid.*, 352.

37   Louis Calaferte, *Septentrion*, op. cit., 417.

38   Jean-René Huguenin, *Journal*, op. cit., 353.

39   Sigmund Freud, "Hysterical Fantasies and Their Relation to Bisexuality" [1908], *Freud on Women: A Reader* (New York; London: WW Norton & Co., 1990).

40 Pierre Assouline, *Simenon* (Paris: Julliard: 1992; rééd. Galli-mard, coll. Folio, 1996). See also his *Autodictionnaire Simenon* (Paris: Omnibus, 2009; rééd. Le Livre de poche, 2011).

41 Melanie Klein, *Envy & Gratitude: A Study of Unconscious Sources* (New York: Macmillan, Inc., 1957) respectively, 181 & 202.

42 *Ibid.*, 211, 231.

43 Françoise Héritier, *Masculin/Féminin I. La pensée de la différence* (Paris: Odile Jacob, 1996; rééd. coll. Poches Odile Jacob).

44 Françoise Héritier, Michelle Perrot, Sylviane Agacinski et Ni-cole Bacharan, *La Plus Belle Histoire des femmes* (Paris: Le Seuil, 2011; rééd. coll. «Points,» 2014) 27.

45 Françoise Héritier, *Masculin/Féminin II: Dissoudre la hiérarchie* (Paris: Odile Jacob, 2002; rééd. coll. Poches Odile Jacob) 23 *(author's emphasis)*.

46 Antonin Artaud, *Selected Writings*, op. cit., 291. Tr. modified.

47 *Ibid.*, 83. On all this I refer to what I developed in *Artaud/Joyce. Le corps et le texte* (Nathan, coll. "Le texte à l'œuvre," 1996) (open access book at the following address: https://hal.science/hal-01421746).

48 Roland Barthes, *Œuvres complètes*, III (Paris: Gallimard, 2002) 100.

49 "Words make love," wrote Breton (*Les Pas perdus*, 1924).

50 On Breton's "magical materialism" & his interest in spiritualist parapsychology, see Jean Starobinski, "Freud, Breton, Myers" [1968], *L'œil vivant II: La relation critique* (Paris: Gallimard, 1970) in particular 338–339.

51 André Breton, *Manifestœs of Surrealism* (Michigan: University of Michigan Press, 1972) 29–30.

52 *Ibid.*, 23 & 38. See also André Breton, Philippe Soupault, *Les Champs magnétiques* [1918] (Paris: Gallimard, coll. Poésie, 1971) préface de Philippe Audoin. [TN] The English edition

of *The Magnetic Fields*, tr. Charlotte Mandell (New York: NYRB, 2020) does not contain Audoin's preface.

53   Commentary by Breton in 1930. Cited by Philippe Audoin in his preface to *Champs magnétiques*, op. cit., 14.

54   Maurice Blanchot, *The Space of Literature* [1955] (Lincoln; London: University of Nebraska Press, 1982) 180 and 50.

55   *Ibid.*, 62.

56   *Ibid.*, 54.

57   *Ibid.*, respectively 184 and 177.

58   [TN] The phonic games Grossman here refers to are not visible or audible in English: *immaculée* (immaculate) contains the word cul (ass) and conception (conception) contains the word *con* (idiot, fool, schmuck, twat, et cetera).

59   [TN] In French, there is a homophony between *naître* (to be born) and *n'être* (not to be, to be nothing) that Breton and Éluard play with, but this is lost in English.

60   André Breton, Paul Éluard, *Immaculate Conception* (London: Atlas Press, 1990) 33 (my emphasis).

61   Julia Deck, *Le Triangle d'hiver* (Paris: Les Éditions de Minuit, 2014) 10.

62   On generative grammar, see for example Noam Chomsky, *Syntactic Structures* (The Hague: Mouton, 1957).

63   Julia Deck, *Le Triangle d'hiver*, op. cit., 20–21.

64   It is sometimes wrong to align the literary experiences of *Stream of Consciousness* of the early 20th century in James Joyce or Virginia Woolf with the inner discourse of a subject. On the contrary, it is the very dissolution of the individual subject *&* of the creative consciousness that arises there. The same turn of the century saw the birth of collective creation experiences from Dada in Zurich, to the Bauhaus in Weimar.

I pursued in *Artaud/Joyce. Le corps et le texte* (op. cit.) the emergence of this writer's fantasy: no longer believing in the fruitfulness of a procreative power contaminated by war and death, and which no longer embody failing fathers and mothers, or a fallen God (become *ape* for Artaud, *noise in the street* for Joyce), he strives to produce in writing an eternally living body-text.

65 Roland Barthes, "The Death of the Author" [1968], *Image, Music, Text* (New York: Hill & Wang, 1977) 143. Tr. modified. For "une impersonnalité créatrice," Stephen Heath has "a prerequisite impersonality."

66 Barthes takes up here the theories of Émile Benveniste who had shown in his work on the system of pronouns and person relations in the verb that "it is in and through language that man constitutes himself as a *subject*…" From this linguistic point of view, "subjectivity" is only "the emergence in the Being of a fundamental property of language. It is 'ego' which says 'ego.'" See "On Subjectivity in Language," *Problems of General Linguistics* (Florida: University of Miami Press, 1971) 223–231.

67 [TN] *Scripteur* is the French noun for the writer of the pope's bulls, hence someone engaged in a writing that is strictly impersonal, someone acting only as an intermediary.

68 Deleuze writes: "In the first place, philosophy isn't just the preserve of philosophy professors. You're a philosopher by becoming one, that is, by engaging in a very special form of creation, in the realm of concepts. Guattari is an amazing philosopher, particularly when he talks about politics, or about music." *Negotiations, 1972–1990* (New York: CUP, 1990) 26.

69 Gilles Deleuze & Félix Guattari, *A Thousand Plateaus* (New York; London: Continuum, 1987) 288. Already in *Logic of Sense* (New York: CUP, 1990), with regard to stoic incorpo-

reality, Deleuze evoked "the 'they' of impersonal and pre-individual singularities, the 'they' of the pure event wherein it dies in the same way *it* rains. The splendor of the 'they' is the splendor of the event itself or of the fourth person." See 152.

70 Gilles Deleuze, *Negotiations*, op. cit., 7.

71 *Ibid.*, 6.

72 Have we noticed enough that *Logic of Sense*, written by Deleuze alone, was also a tribute to Mallarmé's "Coup de dés"? "As on a pure surface, certain points of one figure in a series refer to other points of another figure: an entire galaxy of problems with their corresponding dice-throws, stories, & places, a complex place, a 'convoluted story' — this book is an essay for a logical and psychoanalytic novel." Foreword to *Logic of Sense*, op. cit., xiv.

73 Gilles Deleuze, Claire Parnet, *Dialogues* (New York: CUP, 1987) 13.

74 Gilles Deleuze, *Negotiations*, op. cit., 126.

75 *Ibid.*, 6.

76 On the collapse and the roll of the dice, see Gilles Deleuze, *Difference and Repetition* (New York; London: Athlone Press, 1995) 225–256.

77 "'The relation of this *Autrui* to myself is not a relation of subject to subject.' I admit that in saying and in hearing that, I experienced a feeling of fear: as though we were coming directly up against the unknown [...]." In Maurice Blanchot, *The Infinite Conversation* (Minneapolis; London: University of Minnesota Press, 1993) 70.

78 The two articles originally appeared in the journal *Critique*. The first, from June 1966, was republished in *Dits et Écrits I* (Paris: Gallimard, coll. Quarto, 2001) 546–567. The second, on *Difference & Repetition & Logic of Sense*, from November 1970, was republished in the same collection, 945–967.

79 Gilles Deleuze, Claire Parnet, *Dialogues*, op. cit., 17.

80 Michel Foucault, "The Thought from Outside," *Foucault/ Blanchot*, op. cit., 15 & 19.

81 Michel Foucault, "What is an Author?" [1969], *Language, Counter-Memory, Practice* (New York: Cornell University Press, 1977), op. cit., 132.

82 Michel Foucault, "Theatrum Philosophicum," *Language, Counter-Memory, Practice*, op. cit., 165.

83 At first I thought I read (wrongly?) the mischievous initials of the title, *Logic of Sense* [*Logique du sens*].

84 Michel Foucault, "Theatrum Philosophicum," *Language, Counter-Memory, Practice*, op. cit., 196. Let us note in passing that it was first of all Bouvard and Pécuchet who Foucault described above as "a-categorical beings."

85 Gilles Deleuze, *Negotiations*, op. cit., 138.

86 *Ibid.*, 105 and 83.

87 Maurice Blanchot, *Michel Foucault As I Imagine Him*, op. cit., 107.

88 Michel Foucault, *History of Sexuality II. The Uses of Pleasure* [1984] (New York: Vintage Books, 1985) 8. Let us note in passing the performative enunciation of this sentence which invites, through unfolding, its reader to bewilderment: "What would the relentless pursuit of knowledge *be worth if it were only to secure that* the acquisition of knowledgeableness ..." This 'that' can indeed confuse. One might expect a complete 'that,' introducing a subordinate such as: "secure that the acquisition of knowledgeableness ... is essential ...." We have to turn back to read in fact a restrictive 'that' (not ... only), equivalent to: "if the relentless pursuit of knowledge were to ensure only the acquisition of knowledgeableness ...."

89 See, for example, the opening pages of *The Order of Discourse*, his inaugural lecture at the Collège de France, where he quotes Beckett's *The Unnamable* without naming it.

90 Maurice Blanchot, *Michel Foucault As I Imagine Him*, op. cit., 63.

91 *Ibid.*, 109.

92 Maurice Blanchot, *Friendship* (California: SUP, 1997) 291.

93 Gilles Deleuze, *Negotiations, op. cit.*, 116. Perhaps ironic play also with the masculine stereotype: "brotherhood of arms." [TN] The phonic play in French between "*fraternité d'âme*" (brotherhood of the soul) and "*fraternité d'armes*" (brotherhood of arms) cannot be rendered in English.

94 *Ibid.*, 93.

95 Michel Foucault, *Foucault Live: Collected Interviews, 1961–1984*, ed. Sylvere Lotringer (New York: Semiotext(e), 1989) 313.

96 Gilles Deleuze, *Negotiations,* op. cit., 85.

97 On all this, see *Negotiations,* op. cit., 110; *Foucault,* op. cit., 96–97.

98 Gilles Deleuze, *The Fold,* op. cit., 76–78, 62–63, 115–116.

99 For example here: "The writer [...] possesses an irresistible and delicate health that stems from seeing and hearing things too great for him, too strong for him, suffocating things whose passage exhausts him [...]. From what he has seen and heard, the writer returns with bloodshot eyes and pierced eardrums. What health would be sufficient to liberate life wherever it is imprisoned by and within man, by and within organisms and genera?" In *Essays Critical and Clinical* (New York; London: Verso, 1998) 3.

100 Let us recall the example of Latin grammar: "the fear of enemies" (metus hostium) hesitating between subjective genitive (enemies fear) & objective genitive (we fear enemies). Who fears whom, in fact? Who humiliates whom, in the game of projective identifications?

101 See Pierre Zaoui, *La Traversée des catastrophes* (Paris: Le Seuil: 2010).

102 Antonin Artaud, *Selected Writings*, op. cit., 125.

103 *Ibid.*, 81.

104 [TN] The phonic ambivalence Grossman refers to in Artaud's text concerns the hesitation between *"subi"* (suffered) and *"subit"* (sudden), a subtle traversal that forces the reader to remain vigilant when *experiencing* Artaud's texts. This nuanced chasm cannot be equally rendered in English.

105 Antonin Artaud, *Selected Writings*, op. cit., 23; 31. Translation modified.

106 Edmund Husserl, "Philosophy and the Crisis of European Man," in *The Crisis of the European Sciences and Transcendental Phenomenology* (Evanston: Northwestern University Press, 1970) 299.

107 Antonin Artaud, "Theater and Anatomy," *Watch Fiends & Rack Screams*, tr. by Clayton Eshleman (1995) 45.

108 Antonin Artaud, *The Theater and its Double, op. cit.*, 10.

109 *Ibid.*, 13.

110 Samuel Beckett, *The Unnamable,* in *Three Novels: Molloy, Malone Dies, The Unnamable* (New York: Grove Press, 2009) 375.

111 *Ibid.*, 375.

112 [TN] The French word *assistant* can mean to offer charity (*assister*), to attend or be present for someone, and also spectator, bystander, or assistant. Diderot plays with these meanings in *Salon de 1767* wherein a spectator is so overcome by a painting that he believes he can enter into it and assist in or alter its action.

113 Another example of the same movement of desire-rejection in *Molloy*: "from time to time a co-detainee whom we would like to approach, kiss, milk, breastfeed, and we meet, with bad eyes, for fear that he will allow himself familiarities" (op. cit.) 8.

114 [TN] Here Beckett plays upon the double meaning of "*se sauver*" which means both to "run away" and to "save yourself." This cannot be rendered in English.

115 Samuel Beckett, *The Unnamable,* op. cit., 375–76.

116 [TN] These pseudo-poetic rhymes only function in French (*poème/n'aime; poésie/lit; mot/métro*), as if Beckett had abandoned mimicking in English the parodic birth of poetic rhymes.

117 [TN] Here Grossman uses the French word *ratage*, not *échec*. To denote the active aspect of this condition, the former word is always translated as *failing*, the latter as *failure*.

118 Gilles Deleuze, "The Exhausted," in *Essays Critical and Clinical* (London: New York: Verso, 1998) 152–174.

119 Guy Debord, *The Society of the Spectacle* (New York: Zone Books, 1994) 12.

120 *Ibid.*, 22.

121 See, for example, Jacques Le Rider, "Nietzsche et la France. Présences de Nietzsche en France," in Friedrich Nietzsche, *Œuvres* (Paris: Éditions Robert Laffont: 1993; rééd. coll. Books) XI–CXII. On the links between the thought of Artaud and that of Nietzsche, see Camille Dumoulié, *Nietzsche et Artaud. Pour une éthique de la cruauté* (Paris: P.U.F., 1992).

122 Georges Bataille, *Acéphale*, N° 5 (June 1939), reprinted in *The Sacred Conspiracy* (London: Atlas Press, 2017) 423–24. Translation slightly modified.

123 Friedrich Nietzsche, *The Gay Science,* op. cit., §§ 1, 3, and 4 of Nietzsche's preface.

124 Gilles Deleuze, *Nietzsche & Philosophy* (London: Athlone Press, 1983) 31.

125 Jean Granier, *Le Problème de la vérité dans la philosophie de Nietzsche* (Paris: Le Seuil, 1966) 11.

126 Friedrich Nietzsche, *Human, All Too Human, II. The Wanderer and His Shadow* (Cambridge: Cambridge University Press, 1986; 1996) §67.

127 Nietzsche's emphasis. *The Gay Science*, §351, "In honor of the priestly type."

128 Friedrich Nietzsche, *Thus Spoke Zarathustra*, tr. Graham Parkes (Oxford: Oxford University Press, 2008) Prologue §5.

129 On all this, see Éric Blondel, *Nietzsche: The Body and Culture* (Stanford: Stanford University Press, 1991), in particular 22–41. His analyses fall within the claimed lineage of the work of J. Bollack and H. Wismann's *Héraclite ou la séparation* (Paris: Les Éditions de Minuit, 1972). See also Patrick Wotling, *La Pensée du sous-sol* [1997] (Paris: Allia, 2007).

130 Peter Pütz, "Introduction," in Friedrich Nietzsche, *Œuvres II,* op. cit., 17.

131 Stéphane Mallarmé, "Mystery in Literature," in *Mallarmé in Prose* (New York: New Directions, 2001) 51.

132 *Ibid.,* 50. Translation modified. [TN] In the original text, Mallarmé plays (perhaps) between *"l'ébat de la langue"* (the frolic of language) and *"le débat des grammairiens"* (the debate of grammarians), suggesting a frolic, amorous frolics as Grossman says above, the sensuality of language.

133 On the question of grammar and the order of the world in Nietzsche, see Marc Crépon, "Nietzsche et la question de la langue maternelle," *Cahiers de Herne* "Nietzsche" (2000) 91–92.

134 See Patrick Wotling, *La Philosophie de l'esprit libre. Introduction à Nietzsche* (Paris: Flammarion, 2008), in particular 353–398.

135 Friedrich Nietzsche, *The Gay Science*, Book 5, §347.

136 Gilles Deleuze, Félix Guattari, *What is Philosophy?* (New York: CUP, 1994) 202.

137 Louise Bourgeois, interview with Christiane Meyer-Thoss, cited in the catalogue *Louise Bourgeois*, ed. by Marie-Laure Bernadac and Jonas Storsve (Paris: Centre Pompidou, 2008) 271.

138 Samuel Beckett, "La peinture des van Velde ou le Monde et le Pantalon," *Disjecta* (London: Calder, 1983) 118–132; 123. [TN] For an English translation of this text, see *Hyperion: On the Future of Aesthetics*, Vol. XV, Nº I (Winter 2022) 34–55.

139 Friedrich Nietzsche, *Thus Spoke Zarathustra*, I, "Of the Thousand & One Goals," op. cit., 52.

COLOPHON

THE CREATIVITY OF THE CRISIS
was handset in InDesign CC.

The text font is 205 TF *Louize*.

The display font is DTL *Fleischmann*.

Book design *&* typesetting: Alessandro Segalini

Cover design: CMP, with thanks to Will Scarlett

THE CREATIVITY OF THE CRISIS
is published by Contra Mundum Press.

Contra Mundum Press   New York · London · Melbourne

CONTRA MUNDUM PRESS

*Dedicated to the value & the indispensable importance of the individual
voice, to works that test the boundaries of thought & experience.*

The primary aim of Contra Mundum is to publish translations
of writers who in their use of form and style are *à rebours*, or
who deviate significantly from more programmatic & spurious
forms of experimentation. Such writing attests to the volatile
nature of modernism. Our preference is for works that have not
yet been translated into English, are out of print, or are poorly
translated, for writers whose thinking & æsthetics are in opposition to timely or mainstream currents of thought, value systems,
or moralities. We also reprint obscure and out-of-print works
we consider significant but which have been forgotten, neglected,
or overshadowed.

There are many works of fundamental significance to *Weltlitera-
tur* (& *Weltkultur*) that still remain in relative oblivion, works
that alter and disrupt standard circuits of thought — these war-
rant being encountered by the world at large. It is our aim to
render them more visible.

For the complete list of forthcoming publications, please visit
our website. To be added to our mailing list, send your name and
email address to: info@contramundum.net

Contra Mundum Press
P.O. Box 1326
New York, NY 10276
USA

SOME FORTHCOMING TITLES

AGRODOLCE SERIES ÆD

HYPERION
On the Future of Æsthetics   2006–2023

To read samples and order current & back issues of *Hyperion*,
visit contramundumpress.com/hyperion
Edited by Rainer J. Hanshe & Erika Mihálycsa (2014 ~)

CONTRA MUNDUM PRESS

is published by Rainer J. Hanshe
Typography & Design: Alessandro Segalini
Publicity & Marketing: Alexandra Gold

THE FUTURE OF KULCHUR
A PATRONAGE PROJECT

With bookstores and presses around the world struggling to survive, and many actually closing, we are forming this patronage project as a means for establishing a continuous & stable foundation to safeguard our longevity. Through this patronage project we would be able to remain free of having to rely upon government support &/or other official funding bodies, not to speak of their timelines & impositions. It would also free CMP from suffering the vagaries of the publishing industry, as well as the risk of submitting to commercial pressures in order to persist, thereby potentially compromising the integrity of our catalog.

CAN YOU SACRIFICE $10 A WEEK FOR KULCHUR?

For the equivalent of merely 2–3 coffees a week, you can help sustain CMP and contribute to the future of kulchur. To participate in our patronage program we are asking individuals to donate $500 per year, which amounts to $42/month, or $10/week. Larger donations are of course welcome and beneficial. All donations are tax-deductible through our fiscal sponsor Fractured Atlas. If preferred, donations can be made in two installments. We are seeking a minimum of 300 patrons per year and would like for them to commit to giving the above amount for a period of three years.

WHAT WE OFFER

Part tax-deductible donation, part exchange, for your contribution you will receive every CMP book published during the patronage period as well as 20 books from our back catalog. When possible, signed or limited editions of books will be offered as well.

WHAT WILL CMP DO WITH YOUR CONTRIBUTIONS?

Your contribution will help with basic general operating expenses, yearly production expenses (book printing, warehouse & catalog fees, etc.), advertising and outreach, and editorial, proofreading, translation, typography, design and copyright fees. Funds may also be used for participating in book fairs and staging events. Additionally, we hope to rebuild the *Hyperion* section of the website in order to modernize it.

From Pericles to Mæcenas & the Renaissance patrons, it is the magnanimity of such individuals that have helped the arts to flourish. Be a part of helping your kulchur flourish; be a part of history.

HOW

To lend your support & become a patron, please visit the subscription page of our website: contramundum.net/subscription

For any questions, write us at: info@contramundum.net

www.ingramcontent.com/pod-product-compliance
Lightning Source LLC
Chambersburg PA
CBHW020203090426
42734CB00008B/924